CW00573011

Angels of Light?

Angels of Light?

*The Challenge of
New Age Spirituality*

LAWRENCE OSBORN

Foreword by Lesslie Newbigin

daybreak
London

First published in 1992 by
Daybreak
Darton, Longman and Todd Ltd
89 Lillie Road, London SW6 1UD

© 1992 Lawrence Osborn

ISBN 0–232–51963–3

A catalogue record for this book is available
from the British Library

Cover: design by Sarah John

Phototypeset by Intype, London
Printed and bound in Great Britain at
the University Press, Cambridge

Contents

Part III: The Churches and the New Age

Foreword

Anyone who hopes to understand and cope with the contemporary western world needs to have some understanding of the New Age movement. Its effects are felt in a great many ways, often in a beneficient manner – for example in concern for the environment and in the quest for holistic ways of healing. But it is also not easy to understand. This is partly because it is so pervasive and appears in so many different ways and so many different areas of our common life. It is also because the New Age movement arouses both strong enthusiasms and also powerful revulsions. But, more than this, it is hard for most people to 'get hold of' because it is itself one manifestation of the revolt against the sort of technocratic rationalism which has largely dominated public life in the western world since the Enlightenment. Like the widespread resurgence of religious fundamentalism – though in a very different way – it expresses the revolt of the human spirit against a far too limited understanding of the human capacity to respond to the whole of reality. But once we let go of the kind of rational forms which have shaped public education for so many generations, one is apt to find oneself in an uncharted sea with no clear criteria for deciding what it is rational to believe and what is just nonsense.

Lawrence Osborn has provided for us a set of charts which will, I think, be as helpful to many others as they have been to me. He combines a warm and loving evangelical faith with a very well-equipped mind and a capacity for cool, balanced judgement. He knows New Age from the inside, but he also explores with a quite remarkable thoroughness the complex, deep and ancient roots of the movement in philosophy and religion, both western and eastern, in ancient and modern occultism, in modern psychotherapy and in some of the developments in modern physics and biology. He deals gently but firmly both with those Christians who have accepted too uncritically ideas taken from the New Age, and with those who see New Age simply as an eruption of demonic powers. And he ends with quiet advice to those who wish to enter into a dialogue between the gospel and this particular manifestation of our contemporary culture.

I am tempted to embark on an exploration of some of the fascinating insights which the book opens up, but that would be to go beyond the proper business of a foreword. I would simply commend the book as necessary reading for anyone who wants to understand our contemporary western world, for the ideas of the New Age penetrate into every part of it.

LESSLIE NEWBIGIN
Selly Oak

Acknowledgements

I wish to thank Mr Christian Szurko, Director of Dialogcentre UK. Not only was he willing to spend many hours discussing ideas associated with this project but he demonstrates, in his ministry, the constructive Christian response to new religious movements which I have outlined in the final chapter.

Many other people and institutions have contributed to my research in various ways. In particular I wish to thank Mike and Sally Alsford, Graham Baldwin, Russ Parker, Mike and Kathy Peat, Philip Seddon, and Ian and Margaret Wilson for their prayers. Last but by no means least, it would not have been possible for me to undertake the necessary research without the generous financial assistance of the Whitefield Institute, Oxford.

Introduction:
Encountering the New Age

In the past decade the New Age movement has emerged as a significant factor in western culture. In 1980 it was still possible to dismiss the New Age as part of the lunatic fringe. It was even possible not to encounter it. Today it is hard not to meet aspects of the New Age and it is becoming increasingly difficult not to take them seriously.

I first encountered it twenty years ago as an undergraduate. In those days the term 'New Age' was not used. Nevertheless the heady mixture of esoteric spirituality, pop psychology, and radical politics to which I turned in the early days of my personal spiritual pilgrimage would now be recognized as New Age. I sought meaning and truth in the writings of Richard Bach, Carlos Castaneda, Aleister Crowley, John Lilley, and Louis Pauwels.

However, I became a Christian and left all that behind. Like many who made that transition from one world to another I forgot that the other world existed. I assumed that it had died as the realism of the 1970s replaced the idealism of the 1960s.

I rediscovered the New Age about five years ago while I was doing research on Christian attitudes to the environment. As I studied the environment movement I was fascinated by the rise of deep ecology and Green spirituality. Further investigations revealed that they overlapped with my own spiritual prehistory – now repackaged and with a fashionable new image.

More recently I have been able to devote a good deal of time to studying the New Age movement itself. This book is the fruit of that research. I have tried to understand the New Age in its own terms. But I also seek to analyse the phenomenon and address the question of how Christians should respond to this dramatic spiritual awakening which is going on outside the churches.

This is not merely a local issue. The New Age phenomenon is to be found worldwide. Its extent was brought home forcibly to me just a few months ago during a lecture tour of Romania. Before leaving this country my companion and I consulted an expert on the state of religion in Eastern Europe. We were assured that there was virtually no New Age activity in Romania. On our arrival in the Moldavian city of Suceava that opinion was confirmed by local church leaders. However it took us less than a quarter of an hour in the city centre to find posters advertising New Age events!

The moral of that story is two-fold. First, New Age ideas and activities are now virtually co-extensive with western culture. Wherever people have adopted the values and lifestyle of our culture, you will find New Agers. Cynics have suggested that the New Age is a function of affluence, that it thrives only amongst the wealthy. That is clearly not the case in Romania. Secondly, the New Age is not always easy to recognize. It may be encountered in many ways, and under many different guises.

A word of explanation about the structure of this book is in order. Part I is devoted to describing the most common manifestations of New Age thought. In Part II, I turn my attention to an analysis of New Age beliefs. Finally, in Part III, I explore the interaction between the New Age movement and Christianity. A number of Christian critiques of the New Age take a different approach, beginning with an overview of New Age beliefs. This may help to make sense of a complex phenomenon. However, it may lead to a distorted description of the New Age as the author seeks to illustrate the overview rather than describe the phenomenon. In particular, aspects of New Age belief and practice which do not fit into such an overview may simply be ignored. By describing the phenomenon before attempting to analyse it, I hope to avoid this particular danger.

But before embarking on these explorations, I would like you to join me on a brief journey around some of the British showcases of the New Age movement.

(a) Findhorn: a New Age community

The foremost British New Age community is situated outside the village of Findhorn on a sandy wind-swept peninsula near the town of Forres in Northern Scotland. Findhorn had no particular claim to fame until 1962 when an unemployed hotel manager together with his wife, children, and secretary took up residence on the local caravan site. In those days the site was an unprepossessing piece of waste ground overshadowed by its neighbour RAF Kinloss.

Peter and Eileen Caddy, and their friend Dorothy Maclean, set themselves the task of living entirely on the basis of the guidance received by Eileen from her 'inner voice'. They began by scratching a garden out of the infertile soil of the caravan site. Thirty years on the original garden bears witness to the practical common sense contained in that guidance. Following its advice, Peter Caddy treated the sandy soil with large quantities of seaweed and horse manure. The result was a rich loam which now supports a very fine vegetable garden. In the 1960s, however, they managed to produce some record-breaking plants due reputedly to advice received from nature spirits by Dorothy Maclean.

Gradually a community grew up around them as like-minded people began to hear about the activities of the Caddys. Their reputation spread by word of mouth amongst members of the British esoteric community and the nascent counter-culture.

The arrival of David Spangler in 1971 marked the birth of the community as it now exists. During his three years as a member, Spangler began to develop the educational programme for which Findhorn is now generally known. There was also a gradual shift away from the original authoritarian structure to an oligarchy (the decision-making of the community is vested in a series of managers or focalisers, and a core group). Throughout the 1970s the community expanded rapidly, reaching a peak of about 250 members. This period was also characterized by extensive dabbling in occultism which culminated in the so-called 'crystal incident' of 1978: a large quartz crystal was installed in their meeting hall in order to channel occult energies.

In 1979 Peter Caddy left Eileen and Findhorn in order to 'develop himself by means of a new series of relationships'.[1] With his departure, support for crystal power declined and, after an accident involving the central crystal, the entire experiment was abandoned. However, by this time a number of members (including the present focaliser) had resigned in disgust at the increasingly overt occultism.

The 1980s were a period of retrenchment for the community. It was faced with a massive debt due to its building and land purchase programme. At the same time, its rapid earlier expansion had stretched the capacity of the members' accommodation (mostly caravans and pre-fabricated chalets) beyond a tolerable limit. Under the guidance of a succession of focalisers, membership was gradually reduced to the present level (about 150). More careful financial management has also allowed them to pay off their debts and put them in a strong position for renewed expansion in the 1990s.

Membership does not depend on adherence to a particular set of beliefs. On the contrary, Findhorn is a microcosm of the New Age in the diversity of beliefs expressed by members. That catholicity is reflected in their bookshop: on a recent visit I found not only the usual New Age books but also volumes on Christian spirituality (including a book by the evangelical theologian Francis Schaeffer!).

Human relationships are more important than doctrine at Findhorn. The main criteria for membership are a willingness to be involved in the lives of all who come to the Foundation, a commitment to work thirty hours per week for the community, and readiness to seek a harmonious solution (under the guidance of 'spirit') to any problems which arise. Like all human communities, it has its relationship problems. However, unlike some new religious movements, it is anti-authoritarian: members are free to come and go, to work outside the community, to express their own opinions (even about community leadership). That freedom comes across in the *joie de vivre* evident within the community. Ample opportunities exist for members to engage in creative activities of all sorts.

(b) Glastonbury: a New Age shrine

Unlike Findhorn, the ancient English market town of Glastonbury has a long history of association with the mysterious and
the mystical. The ruined abbey in the town itself and the
remains of the chapel of St Michael on the summit of Glastonbury Tor bear witness to its Christian heritage. Today it is still
a place of pilgrimage but, in addition to Christians, the town
attracts large numbers of New Agers. A stroll down the High
Street will reveal one of the highest concentrations of New Age
businesses outside London. New Age visitors are served by a
variety of New Age bookshops such as *Gothic Image*. They can
find more books as well as all sorts of spiritual and occult
requisites at *Crystal Cave*. If they need healing or therapy of
any kind, the National Federation of Spiritual Healers runs the
local healing centre. Sooner or later most people with an
interest in alternative spiritualities and lifestyles will gravitate
to a courtyard off the High Street where the *Glastonbury
Experience* is based. It is even possible to pick up information
about New Age guest houses offering vegetarian menus and,
perhaps, massage, astrology, or tarot readings.

A major reason for this concentration of New Age activity
in Glastonbury is its connection with the Arthurian legends.
According to legend, the abbey was founded by Joseph of
Arimathea who brought to this ancient holy place the Holy
Grail (the chalice used at the Last Supper). The quest for the
Grail is a central theme of the Arthurian cycle. Glastonbury
itself is often identified with Avalon or *Ynyswytryn* (the Blessed
Isle to which the dying Arthur was brought to find rest). In
fact the connection with Arthur was already so strong in the
thirteenth century that human remains reputed to be those of
Arthur and Guinevere were interred in front of the abbey's
high altar in 1276.

Long before the birth of the New Age phenomenon the
English esoteric community already regarded Glastonbury as a
holy place and the Arthurian legends were venerated as a
source of English wisdom with roots in a pre-Christian past.
As long ago as 1934 the influential occult writer Dion Fortune
devoted an entire book to *Glastonbury: Avalon of the Heart*.

Today occultists and New Agers alike use the Arthurian legends as the basis for guided fantasy exercises. One brochure about the esoteric Glastonbury issues the following appeal to New Agers:

> Whilst Avalon fosters the hope for a Saviour King and the Grail Quest, it also embodies an earlier myth of the potential awakening of the earth goddess, the sleeping titaness . . .
>
> A mandate, as old as these islands, the tale of Hyperboreans and golden apples of eternal life, calls us to this centre of sacred power and wisdom.
>
> Join us in this ancient holy place of great beginnings, this very chalice of renewal.[2]

That appeal is certainly heeded by thousands of people each year. They come to drink in the atmosphere of the place, to make a pilgrimage up the Tor (perhaps ascending by a spiral path as a spiritual exercise), or perhaps to discover for themselves the Terrestrial Zodiac (a vast open-air temple which some esotericists claim to have discerned in the surrounding countryside). In previous years many younger New Agers might have been attracted by the annual Glastonbury Festival. Glastonbury's status as a holy place of the New Age was strikingly confirmed in 1987 by its use as one of the venues for the so-called Harmonic Convergence (a worldwide celebration of a collective shift in the level of human consciousness from tribal to planetary).

(c) The Festival of Mind, Body and Spirit: a New Age event

This festival, which takes place annually in London around the May Bank holiday, is a unique showcase of New Age groups, activities, and therapies, of new religious movements, and of all kinds of alternative spirituality. The New Age is renowned for its directories of alternatives and esoterica. In a very real sense the festival is an incarnation of those directories.

In 1991 over a hundred exhibitors hired stands in the Royal Horticultural Halls. Every conceivable aspect of the New Age was represented from astrological career development to spiritual holidays in Spain and the Aegean. Most of the major New

Age publishers, record companies, and resource centres put on exhibits. A wide range of complementary therapies and diagnostic services were available. Several communities (e.g., Findhorn) and a range of new (or not so new) religious movements (including Christian Spiritualism, Aetherius Society, Theosophy, Baha'i Faith, and Swedenborgianism) were represented. It was possible to buy everything from Tibetan singing bowls, crystals, and magic wands to ginseng, royal jelly, and homoeopathic remedies.

In addition to the exhibits, an important feature of the festival is the range of demonstrations, lectures, and workshops. These enable visitors to get first-hand experience of whatever is currently fashionable in the New Age. Thus it is the perfect place to go window shopping for alternative spiritualities or personal development techniques. In 1991 these ranged from the meditative use of the didgeridoo to concerts of New Age music; from *T'ai Chi Chuan* to circle dancing and eurhythmy; from past life therapy to channelling.

Notably less diverse than the range of exhibits and demonstrations was the range of people who attended. My impression was of a group which was predominantly white and was ready to part with a good deal of money at the various stands. There seemed to be relatively few young or old people there: the bulk would have been in their twenties to forties.

Some longstanding festival goers have started to talk in nostalgic terms of earlier years: the 'good old days' when it was even more diverse. Even allowing for the possibility that it has declined to some extent,[3] the Festival for Mind, Body and Spirit remains the premier showcase for New Age activities in the UK and is an indispensable guide to current trends.

Part I

Aspects of the New Age

1

Transforming the Body:
Holistic Health in the New Age

1. IN PURSUIT OF HEALTH

A characteristic feature of health care today is the dramatic increase in the number of people turning to alternative or complementary therapies. This is reflected in a corresponding explosion in the number of practitioners. This is a much broader movement than the New Age movement. By no means all practitioners would wish to identify themselves with New Age views about reality or New Age hopes for the future of society. In all probability a far lower percentage of their patients would wish to do so. However the New Age movement has espoused the broader complementary health movement to such an extent that the latter has become a major avenue of recruitment for the former.

Two major factors seem to be responsible for the rapid growth of the broader movement. One is the cult of health and beauty within western culture – Hollywood and Madison Avenue seem to have conspired with the mass media to create in our increasingly visual culture an obsession with physical health and beauty. The other is an increasing dissatisfaction with conventional medicine. While there have been dramatic technological advances in health care, these have often been made at great cost. Rightly or wrongly, it is increasingly perceived as concern with technology and cure rather than with the patient as a person. The impersonality of modern medicine fuels fears that hospital treatment has a tendency to dehumanize, if not brutalize, its patients. People also fear that the cure may be little improvement on the original illness: the term *iatrogenic illness* has been coined to highlight the problem of patients developing new (possibly more severe) infections as a result of medical procedures.

An additional factor relates specifically to Christians. It should not be imagined that the holistic health movement is entirely secular in its inspiration or motivation. Christians of all denominations have been in the forefront of developing hospices as a way of countering the perceived brutalization of the terminally ill. There is increasing recognition amongst Christians that the biblical understanding of healing is far broader than physical cure. The account of Jesus' encounter with the woman with the haemorrhage draws a clear distinction between her cure and her healing. In biblical terms, healing has to do with mind, spirit and social relationships as much as with body. Health is closely related to the Old Testament concept of *shalom* – the just peace which characterizes a righteous society.

2. NATURAL REMEDIES

The least controversial aspect of complementary health care is the wide range of alternative (usually natural) medicines that is now available. Many of them are traditional plant preparations (some of which have been used as medical treatments for millenia).

(a) Herbalism

Herbalism has a long and distinguished history. For most of its history western medicine has relied heavily upon herbal remedies. It is really only the past three centuries which have seen a significant divergence between herbalism and conventional medicine. One factor in that divergence was Nicholas Culpepper's efforts to popularize herbalism. While he brought it to a much wider audience, he also tied it closely to astrology at a time when intellectuals were beginning to question astrology. By Victorian times only a tiny minority of medical practitioners relied to any extent upon herbal medicines.

It was the shortage of medicines during World War 1 which resulted in the British revival of herbal medicine. A parallel revival in the United States was spearheaded by the Herb Society of America and by the interest of a number of leading naturopaths (notably Jethro Kloss).

There is nothing specifically New Age about herbalism. Many eminent Christians of previous generations have advocated herbal remedies. For example George Herbert advised would-be clergymen to study herbalism both for its recreational value and in order to meet the medical needs of their parishioners.

However, there has been a definite shift of emphasis within herbalism as a result of the alignment of the New Age with complementary medicine. The role of herbs in curing specific illnesses has been played down in favour of greater emphasis on their role in promoting the total health of the body. Thus a representative of the National Institute of Medical Herbalists can comment that: 'Medical herbalists are concerned with treating the whole person, and not simply relieving symptoms. . . . they assess the causes of ill-health for the individual, and prescribe herbal medicines to help support the person's own healing abilities, and to restore balance.'[1]

Of particular importance is *ginseng*. This is an oriental herbal remedy which has been popularized by contemporary interest in Chinese medicine. To the Chinese it was almost a panacea. In addition to an ability to heal several diseases, they claimed that it prolongs life and increases sexual potency in men. Their high opinion of it has been partially borne out by recent studies which suggest that it may be able to assist in the reduction of stress. Like other herbal remedies there is nothing specifically New Age about the use of ginseng. However some importers have Unification Church connections and Christians may be reluctant to use their products.[2]

(b) Homoeopathy

Like herbalism, homoeopathy used to enjoy a good deal of Christian support.[3] However, it has become controversial as a result of its recent association with the New Age.

Homoeopathy can be traced back to the work of Samuel

Hahneman (1755–1843). The basic principle is based on the observation that many symptoms of disease appear to arise from the body's efforts to resist infection. From this Hahneman concluded that the best medicines operated by exaggerating symptoms rather than suppressing them. More controversial was his belief that very small doses have a more powerful therapeutic effect than large doses. Homoeopathic practitioners regularly operate with solutions which are so dilute that the quantity of the active agent is immeasurably small.

Like herbalism homoeopathy predates the New Age but has been reinterpreted in New Age terms. Specifically the New Age approach to the body provides a framework in which the practice of homoeopathy appears quite rational. Thus New Age homoeopaths may argue that the special process of dilution is designed to eliminate entirely the substance of the active agent while transferring its form or energy to a harmless carrier such as water.[4] Like New Age herbalism, New Age homoeopathy shifts the emphasis of treatment from cure to the achievement of a balance which allows the body's natural healing energies to bring about a total response. Whereas classical homoeopathy focussed on the symptoms of disease the tendency now is to concentrate on the whole person presenting those symptoms.

(c) Aromatherapy

This is most simply explained as a specialized form of herbalism which concentrates on the therapeutic effect of highly concentrated aromatic oils. Like other herbal remedies these have been used therapeutically since antiquity but fell into disuse with the rise of scientific medicine. The modern revival is generally credited to Marguerite Maury, the wife of a French homoeopath.

The oils are used externally usually in the form of skin conditioners or cosmetics, or as massage oils. They are supposed to work either by absorption into the bloodstream through the skin or by direct stimulation of the olfactory system. Practitioners may suggest that they operate on the brain, affecting intuition, memory, emotions, or sex drive.

During the 1980s aromatherapy became very popular

amongst New Agers. Like other forms of herbalism Christian suspicion is largely a matter of guilt by association. The only substantive charges which can be made against the practice is the lack of reliable testing of the remedies and the sometimes extravagant claims which are made for them.

(d) Bach flower remedies

This is a collection of patent medicines devised by Dr Edward Bach as a result of his experiments with herbal remedies. The rationale behind his work was a belief that health was largely a matter of mental state. Thus, in searching for herbal remedies, he focussed on the personality of the patients rather than the symptoms of the disease. His remedies are used to combat the negative emotions which he believed were the true cause of disease and are oriented to the twelve different personality types he recognized.

While the original flower remedies are jealously guarded by the Bach Healing Centre an explicitly New Age version has emerged in the United States. The Flower Essence Society has shifted the emphasis to the role of flower remedies in facilitating the emergence of a New Age consciousness.

3. THE CHINESE DIMENSION

Chinese medicine is increasingly important within the holistic health movement. Many New Agers are attracted to it because of its basis in Taoist philosophy.

(a) Basic concepts

At the heart of Chinese medicine is the Taoist view of reality. This is summarized in the *Tao Te Ching* as follows:

> Tao generates the One
> The One generates the Two
> The Two generates the Three
> The Three generates the Thousand Things[5]

Tao is the Absolute which transcends personality, deity and existence. From it flows *wu-chi*, undifferentiated unity.[6] The One, *wu-chi*, then differentiates into the Two, *Tai Chi*, widely known in the West as *Yin* and *Yang*. These are the polar opposites from which all reality is derived. It leads to a model of the universe in which everything is built around the male-female polarity. Everything is to be understood in terms of the dynamic relationship of *yin* and *yang*.

Integral to the dynamic interplay of *yin* and *yang* is *chi*. Together they constitute the three spoken of in the above quotation. *Chi* is the vital energy which permeates all things; it is the primal creative energy of the universe. It is virtually identical to the Hindu concept of *prana*, and the western concept of psychic energy. *Chi* flows through and nourishes all living bodies.

Finally the dynamic interaction of *yin, yang*, and *chi* is bound up with the five elements of Chinese thought: wood, fire, earth, metal, and water. The interaction can be either creative or destructive: both are necessary for the harmonious balance of the whole.

Chinese medicine is entirely rooted in this view of reality. It assumes that the most basic fact about a living body is that it depends on an unimpeded flow of *chi* through a network of force lines or meridians analogous to the nervous system or circulatory system of western medicine. Thus its diagnostic techniques are directed towards the discovery of imbalances in the flow of *chi*. Similarly, the action of its medicines and therapeutic techniques is understood in terms of improving the flow of *chi* and adjusting the creative and destructive cycles within the body.

(b) Acupuncture

Acupuncture is the best known member of the large family of Chinese therapies. It was introduced into Europe nearly three hundred years ago by a German physician who had spent some time working in Japan. The practice flourished for a while and was even used at Edinburgh Royal Infirmary in the 1830s but gradually fell into disuse during the second half of the nineteenth century.

A number of factors are responsible for its western revival. The Chinese Revolution led to a determination on the part of the Chinese people to present their own medical traditions as the equal of western medicine. Western scientific studies of acupuncture were encouraged. At the same time acupuncture caught the imagination of a variety of practitioners of complementary medicine.

Its use spread to the West for purely pragmatic reasons: at least some people do seem to respond to this treatment (and its use in pain relief is well attested). However, because of its basis in Taoist philosophy it has been accepted most readily by those whose philosophies were compatible with Taoism or who were inclined to view the body in terms of esoteric forces (e.g., astral and etheric bodies).

In classical Chinese medicine the acupuncture points lie on the meridians along which *chi* flows through the body. They are the points at which physical organs are connected to the meridians. It is assumed that in a healthy person *chi* flows freely through these points to nourish all parts of the body. Illness is perceived as a blockage of one or more of these points leading to an imbalance in the flow of *chi*. Inserting needles into these points is believed to remove or reduce the blockage, restoring the natural balanced flow of *chi*.

Acupuncture certainly has some effect though perhaps not as great as is sometimes claimed.[7] However the mechanism is not understood. The classical Chinese explanation does not, in fact, explain *how* acupuncture assists the flow of *chi*. In any case there is no consensus on the number of acupuncture points. If there were a simple direct correlation with physical organs one would expect the number of acupuncture points and the locations to be clearly defined.

(c) Acupressure

This is a variation on acupuncture in which pressure or massage is used instead of needles. Many people believe that it is the older technique and that acupuncture evolved from it. However its spread to the West was hindered by Japanese laws against massage which outlawed it until 1955.

The best known Chinese school of acupressure is *Shen-Tao*. It has spawned a wide range of variant techniques including the Japanese *Shiatsu* and a number of self-applied techniques such as *Do-In* and *Ge Jo*. It has also been amalgamated with *hatha yoga* to produce a technique known as *acu-yoga*.

These techniques are widely used by members of the holistic health movement and also by New Agers. In addition to their therapeutic effect the massage methods of, for example *Shiatsu*, are used as an aid to focusing the mind for meditation or self-development exercises of various kinds.

(d) Western developments

In addition to the many oriental forms of acupuncture and acupressure, the western holistic health movement has generated a number of variations of its own. These include the electrical stimulation of acupuncture points; *osteopuncture* (inserting acupuncture needles into the underlying bone), *auriculotherapy* (acupressure applied to the ear lobes), and *polarity therapy* (which blends acupuncture with chiropractic and naturopathy). Probably the most widely used of these western variants are *applied kinesiology* and *reflexology*.

Applied kinesiology is a development of diagnostic muscle testing which incorporates insights from chiropractic and acupressure. According to its practitioners, poor muscle tone arises from the same clogging of meridians and acupuncture points which is responsible for illness. They believe that improving muscle tone will improve the flow of *chi*. Thus, having mapped the areas of poor muscle tone, a therapeutic regime (consisting of exercise, massage and certain diets) is prescribed in order to strengthen those muscles.

If there is a sound basis for this practice the resultant improvement in muscle tone should have a direct effect in terms of relief from the corresponding illness. In practice, applied kinesiologists tend to emphasize prevention rather than cure.

Some of the diagnostic techniques developed by kinesiology are used by New Agers for a wide range of purposes. For example, a New Age allergy specialist may ask a client to hold samples while stretching out their arm. By applying pressure to the arm the specialist claims to be able to tell the substances to which the client is allergic. You may sometimes see a similar process being used in New Age shops when people are deciding which crystals to buy (the beneficial crystal will supposedly cause a visible strengthening of the arm).

Reflexology developed out of *zone therapy*, which divides the body into ten zones through which vital energy flows, and stresses the therapeutic effect of pressure and massage. In zone therapy the foot is seen as a microcosm of the body because all ten zones begin and end in the hands and feet. Thus foot massage is seen as a very effective way of removing energy blockages from the zones. In effect, reflexology is a specialized form of acupressure applied to the feet.

4. BODY WORK

This is the generic term for a variety of techniques in which the practitioner works directly with the structural elements of the human body, the muscles and bone structure. Some of these techniques are as old as medicine itself and may well be used by conventional medicine as part of the therapeutic process. The term is also applied to a number of practices in which the therapeutic effect is of secondary importance (e.g., *yoga* and the martial arts).

Those forms of body work in which therapy is the main concern may be divided into two types: manipulation and massage. As in the case of herbalism, there is no innate connection between these techniques and the New Age movement. However the importance of New Agers as potential clients means that here too there has been a shift in emphasis away from the therapeutic aspect. Massage, in particular, is now often marketed as an aid to personal transformation.

Anyone who has visited a physiotherapist will be familiar with what is involved in manipulation. However two major schools of manipulative therapy are associated with complementary medicine. *Osteopathy* is a system of manipulation designed to counter the effects of damage to joints, the spinal column and other parts of the body. It was developed by an American army surgeon, Andrew Still, who believed that proper adjustment of the muscles and skeleton was an essential part of the healing process. The other major approach to manipulation is *chiropractic*. This is an offshoot of osteopathy in which the emphasis is on manipulation of the spine.

Massage was widely used by the Greeks and Romans as part of the daily ritual of the public baths. Perhaps because of its association with the immorality of that institution it fell into disuse with the rise of Christendom and only returned in the sixteenth century. The term 'massage' was coined in nineteenth century France but the practice was already well-established in Britain under the more prosaic title of 'medical rubbing'. It is widely recognized as an enjoyable form of relaxation with possible therapeutic benefits.

(a) Rolfing

I first came across rolfing as an unexplained reference in Marilyn Ferguson's *Aquarian Conspiracy*. She cites it as one way in which people have achieved altered states of consciousness. I was surprised to discover that *structural integration* or *rolfing* (after its creator Ida Rolf) is a form of therapeutic manipulation which focusses on the deep connective tissue between bone joints.

Rolf's starting-point was the observation that, unlike most other animals, humans have adopted an upright posture. This is less stable but more dynamic and flexible than going on all fours. She also stressed an insight from classical mechanics, namely, that the moment of inertia decreases as the mass of a rotating body is moved towards its axis of rotation (hence skaters and dancers achieve fast spins by pulling their arms in towards their centre of gravity). This was the basis for her belief that a body properly aligned vertically with respect to gravity is more efficient than one which is imbalanced in some way.

In reality, however, most of us are not so aligned. Many factors conspire to create slight distortions in our posture.

These include accidents (even quite minor ones), bad habits (possibly learned from parents), environmental factors (e.g., ill-fitting shoes or desks of the wrong height), and emotional factors (e.g., stress). As the body compensates for these distortions the connective tissue between certain joints is put under permanent tension. Our posture may feel natural but that is because we have adapted to an unnatural posture.

According to Rolf, the effect of bad posture is wide-reaching. Our body becomes less efficient. Muscles are forced to take on the load-bearing function of bone. In the long term, postural defects begin to have a deleterious effect on the circulation as well as on the location and function of organs in the body.

Rolf's approach was to restore the plasticity of the body's connective tissue by means of deep massage and manipulation. The full programme consists of ten hour-long (and, at times, acutely painful) sessions. Once the tissue is freed in this way the body is expected to return naturally to its proper alignment. Subsequently the patient may follow a sequence of exercises developed by Judith Aston in order to maintain the restored plasticity.

Because some aspects of bad posture may be related to emotional and psychological factors, rolfing may take on a counselling dimension. Patients may find that associated with the pain and the new-found freedom of movement there is a powerful emotional release. In some cases, patients have reported significant spiritual experiences during these sessions.

Rolfing was taken up early on by the New Age movement. This is probably because Ida Rolf regularly taught her techniques at the Esalen Institute during the 1960s. As you might expect the holistic aspect of the therapy is an important factor in this association.

Rolfing itself is not widely used in the UK. However there are a number of practitioners of very similar techniques such as *postural integration* and *Hellerwork*.

(b) Feldenkrais method

This form of body work was developed by a Jewish physicist, Moshe Feldenkrais, in response to a sports injury sustained as a young man. Rather than face surgery and possible permanent disability he made an extensive study of neurophysiology, acupuncture, yoga, and the martial arts in order to teach himself to walk in spite of the injury. Subsequently he developed his discoveries into a full-scale therapeutic technique. It was widely popularized by his successful work with a number of eminent people including the Israeli politician, David Ben-Gurion, and the musician, Yehudi Menuhin.

Fundamental to the system is the belief that movement, sensation, feeling, and thinking are neurologically inseparable. Health depends on proper organization of the nervous system and the most direct way of tackling that is through refining the ability to move. Conversely much pain and physical disability is the result of inappropriate learning. Thus by teaching clients new and more appropriate ways of moving the Feldenkrais practitioner can help them overcome physical disabilities and improve not only their physical health but also their psychological health.

Like rolfing, the connection with the New Age has much to do with the holistic emphasis on the interrelationship of body and mind, and also on the fact that Feldenkrais taught at Esalen during the early 1970s.

5. HEALING THROUGH MIND AND SPIRIT

The holistic perspective in complementary medicine has been a recurring feature throughout this chapter. So far, we have simply noted that the remedies and physical therapies on offer make claims beyond the merely physical. Improvement of physical health is perceived to have psychological and spiritual benefits.

But the converse is also true. A number of psychological and spiritual techniques are on offer which claim to have direct physical benefits.

(a) Biofeedback

This well-known technique involves allowing the patient to monitor certain body functions. The rationale behind it is that we can learn to control certain normally autonomous aspects of the way our body works. It provides us with the opportunity for conscious mental control of, e.g., heart rate, blood pressure, skin temperature or brain waves.

Biofeedback devices of various sorts are certainly used by New Agers but the technique is widely used beyond the New Age movement. It can be of real positive benefit in stress reduction, in the control of migraine attacks, and in pain control.

Its condemnation by some Christians as an occult New Age practice is yet another example of guilt by association. The fact that some people use the technique to achieve mystical states is no more an argument against its responsible therapeutic use than, say, the existence of glue sniffing is against the proper use of glue!

(b) Creative visualization

This terms refers to the practice of mentally visualizing a desired state of affairs or some symbolic representation of that state. It may be regarded as the imaginative analogue of positive thinking. In relation to illness, it is claimed that by imagining one's illness in some objective form we can gain control over it, alleviate its symptoms, and even heal ourselves.

The therapeutic use of imagination has a very long history in western medicine. At the Temple of Epidaurus in ancient Greece, patients were encouraged to dream dreams in which a god would appear with advice on the treatment of the illness. During the Renaissance Paracelsus believed that negative emotions were a cause of illness and that we could use our imaginations to overcome those emotions.

Such practices were effectively suppressed by the success of conventional mechanistic medicine and the pervasive mind-body dualism which has dominated western thought since the Enlightenment. However, the re-emergence of a more holistic approach to the relationship between mind, body and spirit has opened the doors to such techniques.

The most dramatic work on the medical applications of visualization has been done by Carl Simonton of the University of Oregon Medical School. He taught visualization techniques to patients with terminal cancer. Out of 159 people who were expected to live less than a year, 63 were still alive four years later (though only 14 had no signs of cancer). Those who died survived on average 50 per cent longer than the members of a control group.

Simonton did not present this technique as a substitute for conventional therapy. Rather, he offered it as a way of encouraging the patients to see their conventional treatment in a more positive light. For example, they might be encouraged to imagine radiotherapy as a hail of tiny energy bullets piercing everything in their path but killing only cancer cells.

The rationale for his use of visualization was the observation that patients with an optimistic outlook tended to respond better to treatment. Visualization, or positive imaging, was chosen as the technique because of his then-wife's studies of highly-motivated, highly-successful individuals, many of whom made use of such techniques.

Visualization is at the very heart of the contemporary debate about the extent of the effect of mental states upon physical health. There is some evidence to suggest that psychological factors may affect the body's immune system. For example Dr David McClelland of Boston University has shown that changes in emotional state can increase (or decrease) the levels of a specific antibody against infections such as colds and flu.[8] Such observations are the basis of the infant science of psychoneuro-immunology. However, the mechanism involved is not yet understood and the extent of the effect is still disputed.

Meanwhile, within the New Age community, the apparent success of positive imaging has encouraged widespread experimentation with related techniques.

(c) Spiritual healing

Perhaps the most controversial aspect of New Age therapies is the increased interest in spiritual healing. This class of techniques appears in two main forms, is known by a variety of names[9] and may differ in detail from healer to healer. However there are certain common features.

The better known form is *contact healing*. This is the practice of the laying-on-of-hands (usually accompanied with prayer or some analogous mental discipline). Healer and patient are in the same place and physical contact (or near contact) is established.

What is believed to happen depends very much on the worldview of the healer. Some see themselves as agents of God or the divine. Others regard the contact as an opportunity for the transference of psychic energy (or *chi*) from the healer to the patient thus strengthening the patient. Yet others see it as a catalytic action, stimulating the patient's own healing processes.

The other form of spiritual healing is *distance healing*. As the name suggests, the patient may be many miles from the healer. It may be as simple as prayer or a visualization process (e.g., imagining a laser beam of light and love penetrating the person seeking help). Alternatively the healer may use contact with something belonging to the patient (or with a surrogate).

An oriental form of spiritual healing (*Reiki* or *The Radiance Technique*) is also practised by western New Agers. It was developed at the beginning of the century by a Japanese Christian minister, Mikao Usui. Unable to find any satisfactory teaching on the Christian healing ministry, he turned to Buddhist texts and, through reading and meditation, activated his own healing powers.

Reiki is structured hierarchically with four degrees of practitioner. However, at the basic levels, its healing techniques are not dissimilar to those of western spiritual healing. A first degree practitioner will be taught the basic skills of laying-on-of-hands (which is understood as a way of channelling *chi* from the healer to the patient). As you progress up the hierarchy you learn more sophisticated techniques including distance healing and techniques for emotional and spiritual healing.

Training for a Reiki master is directed more towards personal growth and enlightenment.

6. THE OCCULT DIMENSION OF HEALING

(a) Crystal therapy

Crystals have become one of the identifying symbols of the New Age. However, they have long been associated with magic and medicine.

According to New Agers crystals are able to accumulate, store, and release at the owner's request spiritual or psychic energy. Different kinds of crystal impose different qualities on this energy. For example, rose quartz is supposed to emit soft soothing energy suitable for healing old emotional hurts whereas citrine is more suited to healing the physical body.

Literature on crystals often gives the impression that such assertions are based on scientific studies. However, the therapeutic effects claimed by crystal therapists can only be understood in the context of a belief system which can accommodate spiritual energies.

(b) Colour therapy

Conventional science accepts that light has a number of beneficial physiological effects, e.g., the production of vitamin D and the stimulation of red blood cell production. In addition, psychologists have observed that different colours can have marked effects on a person's mental state.

However, colour therapy as it has evolved within the New Age has more to do with occult theories of colour and certain eccentric theories about glandular activity than with the conventional wisdom of the scientific establishment.

One of the pioneers of colour therapy, Corinne Heline, correlated different colours with the signs of the zodiac. She believed that illnesses could also be correlated with astrological signs in this way. In her system, the casting of a horoscope was an integral part of the process. By analyzing the illness astrologically it was possible to prescribe exposure to light of certain colours.

(c) Diagnostic divination

Astrology was at one time a very important diagnostic tool. In the Middle Ages, it was believed that the astrologer could answer any question by casting a horoscope for the exact moment when it was asked. The historian Keith Thomas notes that, 'If the question was a medical one the patient might accompany it with a sample of his urine; the astrologer then based his answer upon his interpretation of the sky at the moment when the urine had been voided, or when it had arrived at his consulting-room'.[10]

Another form of divination which is sometimes used for medical diagnosis is *dowsing*. For diagnostic purposes a pendulum is used rather than the traditional forked twig. By holding it over the patient or a sample, the pendulum may indicate by its swing causes and potential remedies. Thus a New Ager might use a pendulum to help him or her in choosing the most appropriate homoeopathic medicine from a display in a shop. This form of dowsing is sometimes known by the name *radiesthesia*.

2

Transforming the Mind:
Psychoanalysis and the New Age

1. FREUD AND THE BEGINNINGS OF PSYCHOANALYSIS

Recent attempts to explore the mind have called into question
the dominance of reason which has been characteristic of western culture. The doubts raised by psychoanalysis are fundamental to New Age understandings of human nature and knowledge. Indeed it would not be an exaggeration to say that the
New Age phenomenon is intimately related to the development
of psychoanalysis during the twentieth century.

The story of psychoanalysis begins with Sigmund Freud
(1856–1939). However, while he was undoubtedly the father of
psychoanalysis, he seems an unlikely precursor for a spiritual
movement such as the New Age.

Freud was avowedly atheistic. Like many thinkers of his
generation he believed that God is a projection of the human
psyche: specifically, he believed that God was the collective
projection of our feelings of guilt in relation to our fathers.
Closely related to this was his notion of conscience as part of
the psyche rather than the voice of God: it became the
aggression of the *superego* (an internal censor constructed from
parental and societal demands) towards the *ego* (the conscious
rational subject). Freud further believed that the projection of
our guilt feelings to create God and conscience was inherently
harmful. Thus religion was for him the psychopathology of
society. As if that were not enough, he demonstrated an
irrational antipathy towards spiritual matters in a memorable
encounter with Carl Jung.[1]

(a) The unconscious

Prior to Freud, western thought tended to identify the psyche with the conscious rational subject. Memory was regarded as a function of consciousness and dreams were largely ignored.

Freud's single most important contribution to the study of the mind was his proposal that beyond the horizons of consciousness lay as yet unexplored dimensions of the mind, psychic *terra incognita*. He was drawn to this conclusion by the observation that strange entities sometimes cross the horizon to disturb our conscious mind. They may come in the form of dreams and fantasies; or they may take a more frightening form – unexplained obsessions, fears, or other irrational urges (irrational, precisely because they are perceived to come from beyond that inner horizon).

Freud began the work of opening up this new territory. However, he retained the Enlightenment insistence on the dominance of the ego. Thus he could only envisage the unconscious as a kind of reservoir for memories, experiences, and emotions that had somehow dropped out of consciousness. It was also a repository for those instincts which were not socially acceptable. For him, the unconscious was a garbage dump of forgotten memories and repressed experiences which sometimes come back to haunt us.

(b) Repression and the function of analysis

Freud proposed the mechanism of *repression* as one way in which we handle painful experiences or unacceptable drives. If we deny the experience or urge with sufficient force, we may drive it down into the unconscious: we have repressed it. However, there is a price to pay. Such material is a major source of psychological disturbance.

Alternatively we may succeed in rechannelling the drive in a positive way. This process of psychic judo is known as *sublimation* and was fundamental to Freud's understanding of creativity.

The psychoanalyst offers a third way of handling such material. Freud experimented with a number of devices for gaining access to the unconscious of his patients. After early work with hypnosis, he concentrated on dream analysis and free association. In the former, the patient would report his dreams to the analyst who would examine the account for images which may have been evoked by unconscious memories. In the latter, the patient is encouraged to speak at random with the minimum of guidance from the analyst. By encouraging the patient to drop his critical faculties in a secure environment, this technique disarms the superego so that snippets of information may leak out of the unconscious without being subject to the usual censorship.

By gaining access to repressed material in a gradual and controlled fashion, the analyst enables the patient to accept it and consciously integrate it into his or her self-image. Negatively, the ghosts of repression are laid to rest. Positively, the experience helps to strengthen the patient's ego.

(c) Freud's contributions to the New Age

In spite of his antipathy, Freud's pioneering work has left its mark on the New Age. Above all, his concept of the unconscious was, through Jung, to become a fundamental part of New Age understandings of human nature.

Dream analysis had long been an accepted part of esoteric traditions. It also has a long (though chequered) history within Christianity. However, prior to Freud, the dominant worldview in the West dismissed dreams as irrelevant or illusory. That negative assessment of dreams is still present to some extent in Freud's work: they were primarily a mine of repressed memories. Nevertheless, his use of dreams as a major tool of analysis gave them a degree of legitimacy which they had not enjoyed for centuries.

Some of Freud's comments on the effects of repression have also had a significant impact on the New Age. He believed that repression could have physical repercussions and that the release of energy associated with overcoming repression would be experienced as an explosive release of tension. The connection between psychic repression and physical tension was to become a fundamental part of Wilhelm Reich's approach to psychoanalysis. Through Reich, Freud has made a significant impact on many of the forms of body work associated with the New Age.

A more subtle contribution is Freud's use of myth. Freudian psychoanalysis is attractive not because it is scientific but because it is expressed mythologically. Far from explaining ancient myths (such as the Oedipus legend) he actually constructed new myths. In doing so he invested unacceptable urges (e.g., to commit incest or suicide) with the dignity of tragedy.[2] In other words he offers the patient imaginative ways of reinterpreting their experience: healing myths. Again through Jung, this positive use of mythology was to have a profound impact on the evolution of the New Age.

2. JUNG: INTO THE UNCONSCIOUS

Carl Gustav Jung (1875–1961) is a much more obvious candidate as a forerunner of the New Age than his some-time associate, Freud. His openness to spiritual experiences of all kinds stands in sharp contrast to Freud's atheism and contempt for spirituality.

(a) Jung's career

On leaving medical school in 1900, Jung took up an appointment at the Burghölzli Psychiatric Clinic in Zurich. During this period he completed his doctoral thesis, 'On the Psychology and Pathology of So-called Occult Phenomena'. It was based on observations of seances conducted by a relative who was a spirit medium. In it he anticipated several themes which were to be developed in his later work. These included the belief that the unconscious was more than a repository of repressed experiences: that it was autonomous of the conscious subject, and played an active role in the development of the personality. He also suggested that the 'spirits' contacted by the medium were aspects of the medium's own unconscious, seeking integration. Generalizing from this, he suggested that psychological disturbances are a natural part of the psyche's quest for wholeness rather than illnesses.

He made the acquaintance of Sigmund Freud in 1906. Their association was to dominate the second phase of his career from 1907 to 1912. For five years Jung was the darling of Freud's circle and Freud himself regarded Jung as his successor, his adopted son. However, what began as mutual admiration rapidly turned sour. Freud began to see Jung as a threat to his dominance of psychoanalysis. Jung, for his part, felt uncomfortable with Freud's marital arrangements and his unreasoning rejection of matters spiritual.

The final break came in 1912 with the publication of Jung's *Symbols of Transformation*. He argued (against Freud) that an exclusively subjective, biographical approach to the symbolism of the psyche was inadequate. He suggested that dreams and fantasies were part of the psyche's process of self-regulation. Most important he proposed that their interpretation should be based on mythology rather than the personal history of the patient.

The next phase of his career was ushered in by several years of profound psychological disturbance as he pursued his mythological approach to the psyche. Jung himself said of that period,

> An incessant stream of fantasies had been released, and I did my best not to lose my head but to find some way to understand these strange things. I stood helpless before an alien world; everything in it seemed difficult and incomprehensible. I was living in a constant state of tension; often I felt as if gigantic blocks of stone were tumbling down upon me. One thunderstorm followed another. My enduring these storms was a question of brute strength. Others have been shattered by them – Nietzsche, and Hölderlin, and many others. But there was a demonic strength in me, and from the beginning there was no doubt in my mind that I must find the meaning of what I was experiencing in these fantasies. When I endured these assaults of the unconscious I had an unswerving conviction that I was obeying a higher will, and that feeling continued to uphold me until I had mastered the task.[3]

There followed the most productive years of Jung's life. In addition to a flourishing private practice he continued his researches and gradually built a new reputation for himself as Freud's rival. In 1921 *Psychological Types* was published: a book which has been very influential not just in psychoanalysis but also in the areas of Christian spirituality and pastoral theology. Another important year for Jung was 1927: the year his association with the sinologist Richard Wilhelm (and, hence, his interest in Taoist alchemy) began.

In 1947 he retired to the tower he had built at Bollingen. The last fifteen years of his life were spent reworking old papers and finishing off a number of major writing projects. Some of his best known works come from this final period (including *Aion, Synchronicity, Answer to Job*, and *Mysterium Coniunctionis*).

(b) Jung's map of the psyche

Jung's concept of the psyche may be pictured as a sphere with a bright field on its surface. The bright field represents consciousness and its centre is the *ego*, the subject. The self is both the nucleus and the whole sphere. Everything apart from the bright field belongs to the realm of the unconscious.[4]

(i) *Jung and the unconscious:* Jung agreed with Freud that the conscious mind attempts to bury in the unconscious all that it is not prepared to face. There is a hinterland just beyond the horizon which is populated by escapees from consciousness. Jung called this the *personal* unconscious.

But he did not believe that this was a complete account of the unconscious. On the contrary, his work on dream analysis and comparative mythology convinced him that some of the entities which emerge from the unconscious cannot be adequately explained in terms of the patient's personal history. Jung cites a dramatic example from his own experience – a mental patient once confided in him a particularly bizarre vision; some years later Jung acquired a recently edited Mithraic liturgy in which that same vision was described. Further investigation revealed analogous ideas and myths in late classical and early mediaeval philosophy and art.[5]

This led him to postulate the existence of a region of the psyche lying beyond the hinterland of the personal unconscious. Unlike the personal unconscious, it is the common heritage of every man and woman. It results not from our personal history but from the inherited possibility of psychic functioning. This is the much misunderstood *collective unconscious*.

It is often interpreted in terms of eastern mysticism. Thus, changing metaphors for a moment, the collective unconscious is seen as the ocean of spirit, and the myriads of individual personalities are merely waves thrown up from the ocean for a brief period. Jung did not see it in that way. At one point he says, 'The collective unconscious contains the whole spiritual heritage of mankind's evolution, born anew in the brain structure of every individual'.[6] This suggests that it is the fundamental genetic programming of the psyche rather than some mystical substratum interconnecting every human consciousness. In other words, our psyches share certain common features just as most human beings have one head, two arms, ten fingers, etc. It is collective in the sense that it is common to all of us rather than that there is only one of it.

But how are we to study this common unconscious? Jung turned to the symbolic contents of dreams, art, mythology, fairy stories, legends, and religious texts. He sought out basic similarities running through these diverse sources; similarities from which he could infer some of the contours, the inner dispositions, of the collective unconscious.

(ii) *The archetypes:* Jung named these inner dispositions *archetypes*. They are the hidden patterns which shape our psychic life.

They remain hidden but their effects are visible in the form of symbolic motifs and images. Analytical psychologists often speak of *archetypal images*, i.e., images which have been brought into being by the archetypes. Jung was careful to stress the distinction. The images belong to the realm of consciousness and, as such, cannot be inherited.

In order to explain the archetypes, Jung related them to instincts. For example he suggested that they were the psychic patterns underlying instinctive behaviour.[7] However, as with all analogies, there are differences as well as similarities. Thus 'while instincts are natural impulses expressed as regular and typical modes of action/reaction, archetypes are dominants which emerge into consciousness from unconsciousness as ideas and images that can be shaped and changed'.[8]

Archetypes are immeasurably more powerful than instincts for, says Jung, 'All the most powerful ideas in history go back to archetypes'.[9] This sometimes startling power of the archetype may create the impression of encounter with another entity. Such experiences may be deeply moving or terrifying; they may be life-changing in their intensity. Many Jungians regard them as explaining traditional accounts of spiritual experience and demonic possession.

(c) The process of individuation

Jung was not content merely to map the contents of the collective unconscious. He also saw a recurring pattern in the order in which the archetypes impinge upon consciousness. This is the point at which my geographical analogy breaks down – it is too static. The psyche is as much a process as a place. Jung called this the *process of individuation*.

But what is the process? Why does the unconscious affect the conscious mind in this way? What is the purpose of dreams and fantasies? Jungians believe it is the process by which the psyche matures.

The ego is not the guiding centre of the process; it does not direct us to maturity. Rather the centre lies in the collective unconscious. This is what Jung calls the *Self*. From that inner centre comes the impulse which drives the psyche towards self-realization. The ego is merely the conscious agent of that impulse.

The task of the ego is to bring to light the hidden potentialities of our psyche under the guidance of the Self. This is achieved by giving up control to the unconscious Self: 'in order to bring the individuation process into reality, one must surrender consciously to the power of the unconscious, instead of thinking in terms of what one should do, or of what is generally thought right, or of what usually happens'.[10]

(i) *The beginning of individuation:* Individuation tends to begin in early adulthood following the normal childhood development of the ego. It is usually triggered by some kind of injury to the personality which amounts to a call from within but is often not recognized as such. Instead it may be put down to external circumstances or it may be experienced as a pervasive *ennui*, a sense of meaninglessness. In effect it is a growing awareness of one's inner contradictions calling us to seek to reconcile those contradictions.

(ii) *The Shadow:* As we respond to that call, the archetype we are most likely to encounter is the *Shadow*. This is the negative image of our conscious personality. It is largely composed of the contents of the personal unconscious – all those repressed experiences, thoughts, and desires. It also represents the unknown and neglected qualities and attributes of the ego.

Often we are more likely to see these qualities in others than in ourselves. We project what we deny in ourselves onto others – particularly those we dislike. However, the first task of individuation, like the first step towards becoming a Christian, is to recognize that those faults lie in us. We must acknowledge the beam in our own eye; we must recognize our own sinfulness. For most people individuation begins by recognizing and owning the shadow-side of our personality.

But there the resemblance with Christianity ends. For the Christian, the shadow, our fleshly nature, must be acknowledged and handed over to crucifixion with Christ. For the Jungian, the shadow must be acknowledged, its strengths assessed, and consciously assimilated. The Jungian theologian Jim Garrison asserts that 'evil cannot be overcome; it works in the psyche to complement the good and should be understood to be as positive a factor as good'.[11]

Jung simply accepted everything he found within the unconscious. His was an empirical approach. From a Christian perspective it is also a disturbingly amoral approach: good and evil are not absolute opposites but polar opposites, i.e., they are interdependent. The tension between them is part of the motive force of individuation. Furthermore, evil is simply unrecognized good: the unacknowledged attributes of the psyche. Our negative attitude to evil is merely fear of the unknown. In the fairy story 'Beauty and the Beast', the beautiful young heroine learns to love the monster. When, at last, she can express her love with a kiss the monster is transformed into a handsome prince. So it is, say the Jungians, with our shadow, our fleshly nature.

(iii) *The anima/animus:* Conscious assimilation of the shadow prepares us to encounter the next major archetype. For men it is the *anima*, for women the *animus*. The anima (animus) is the personification of all the tendencies in a man (woman) which are conventionally regarded as feminine (masculine).

This may vary from culture to culture. In the UK it would include such things as vague feelings and moods, intuitions and hunches, receptiveness to the irrational, capacity for love, and affinity to nature.

In many cultures it also includes the capacity to relate to the divine. This last element appears in Jung's description of the anima as the capacity to relate to the unconscious. Thus she (he) is our guide to the inner world of the collective unconscious.

(b) The Self and God

When we have struggled sufficiently long and seriously with the anima (or animus) we come at last to the encounter with the Self.

When Jung speaks of the Self it is clear that we are again in theologically sensitive territory. He identifies it with the image of God in man, e.g., 'It is only through the psyche that we can establish that God acts upon us, but we are unable to distinguish whether God and the unconscious are two different entities. Both are borderline concepts for transcendental contents.' This sounds as if he is identifying God with the unconscious; a move which could justify the view that there is only one collective unconscious in which we all partake. However, he adds, 'The God-image does not coincide with the unconscious as such, but with a special content of it, namely the archetype of the self. It is this archetype from which we can no longer distinguish the God-image empirically'.[12]

Jung is not trying to say that the Self is divine though many people read him in this way (e.g., Garrison understands individuation as 'the realization of the Self, that is to say, God. The ultimate meaning in life is therefore understood as the realization of the "divine" within us'[13]). Rather, it is the archetype of the Self which gives rise to all the imagery and symbolism by which we attempt to speak to God. For example, a fundamental symbol of the Self is the notion of quaternity. This finds worldwide use as a symbol of wholeness, e.g., the four elements, four temperaments, and four causes in classical and mediaeval philosophy. The circle is another such symbol. Divide the circle in four and you have an equal-armed cross. Elaborate it a little and you have a *yantra* (a mandala, or magic circle, used in tantric yoga as an instrument of contemplation).

(e) Analytical psychology and the New Age

I have described Jung's ideas at some length because of their profound influence on the development of the New Age movement.[14] Before moving on to more recent developments, it is worth highlighting some specific examples of that influence.

(i) *The legitimation of divination:* Jung was fascinated by the phenomenon of the psychologically significant coincidence (*synchronicity*). As part of the research for his theory of synchronicity he carried out astrological studies of some 400 marriages. What he discovered was a statistically significant correlation between the birth charts of the partners. Earlier he had been introduced to the Chinese divinatory technique of the *I Ching* through his interest in Chinese philosophy. This too he found fascinating:

> I would sit for hours . . . the *I Ching* beside me, practising the technique by referring the resultant oracles to one another in an interplay of questions and answers. All sorts of undeniably remarkable results emerged – meaningful connections with my own thought processes which I could not explain to myself.[15]

His own explanation for the phenomenon was the one eventually developed in his theory of synchronicity: that there is a parallelism which relates events which are not physically connected. An alternative explanation found amongst psychological reinterpretations of divination is that the complex pattern produced (whether a birth chart, a cast of yarrow stalks, or the leaves in a tea cup) enables the interpreter's unconscious to make connections. But whatever the explanation of the phenomenon, there can be no doubt that Jung's use of divination has been a major factor in granting such techniques a certain legitimacy which they did not previously possess.

(ii) *The psychologization of spirituality:* Jung was unusually well-versed in the literature of alchemy both western and eastern. He did not practise the art of turning lead into gold. Instead he ransacked the literature for symbolism which would be of use in his interpretation of dreams. He came to believe that the true goal of alchemy and psychoanalysis was one and the same; that the quest for a technique to produce gold was symbolic of a spiritual quest. The Jungian analyst, Vera von der Heyt, comments, 'Analytical psychology today is the heir of alchemy; it is an attitude, a way of seeing, a recognition that whatever is darkest and vilest can be transformed into the highest value'.[16]

This equation of alchemy and analysis is one example of what has become a very widespread approach to spirituality amongst New Agers. Jung was one of the founders of a tradition of reinterpreting spiritual disciplines in psychological terms. This process of psychologization enables modern secular westerners to engage in spiritual disciplines without feeling any embarrassment. It is a major factor in the New Age reappropriation of all kinds of spiritual practices.

3. HUMANIZING PSYCHOLOGY

(a) Wanted: a third force in psychology

American psychology in the late 1940s was entirely dominated by two mutually antagonistic schools of thought neither of which offered much scope for an interest in human spirituality.

On the one hand there was an increasingly arid Freudian psychoanalysis. Freud's disciplines were locked into a reductionistic approach to human behaviour which attempted to interpret it entirely in terms of human sexuality. The limitations of such an approach are immediately obvious when applied to human creativity: while it is true that some art is the result of sublimated sexuality this is ultimately a stultifying view of creativity.[17]

The alternative was an even more arid behaviourism. This was an entirely materialistic approach to psychology which denied any relevance to mental processes. It was interested only in the observable features of human behaviour.

Jung's approach offered a way out of this dilemma but it was too scholarly to have much direct impact on popular thought. If Jung's approach was to reach a wider audience some popularizing force was needed.

(b) Abraham Maslow and humanistic psychology

That third force emerged with the work of Abraham Maslow (1908–70). He became Professor of Psychology at Brandeis University in 1952 and two years later began his campaign to break the dominance of behaviourism with the publication of *Motivation and Personality*. At about the same time he began to build up a network of contacts with other psychologists who were dissatisfied with reductionist explanations of human nature. His book served notice that a much more optimistic view was being unveiled in which the emphasis would no longer be on the pathological states of the human mind. Instead Maslow wanted psychology to develop its understanding of the healthy psyche. He wanted it to concentrate upon healthy, successful and creative individuals (whom he called *self-actualizers*).

(i) *A hierarchy of needs:* Maslow's research into the psychology of healthy individuals revealed a number of requirements for psychological well-being. These he organized into his well-known hierarchy of needs. The most basic level are our physiological requirements such as nourishment and sleep. Next is our need for physical security (an environment with some degree of stability and order). Above that are certain social requirements. We need to belong, to have family and friends. We also need to be valued (by ourselves and others):

because the Protestant work ethic is still strong in America, this is often interpreted as a need for achievement. At the top of the hierarchy Maslow put a need for self-actualization, which he defined as 'the full use and exploitation of talents, capacities [and] potentialities'.[18]

(ii) *Peak experiences:* Maslow observed that the people he denoted as self-actualizers often reported experiences which would once have been characterized as religious: experiences in which values such as wholeness, perfection, completion, justice, simplicity, goodness, beauty, or truth are realized. He called these *peak experiences*.

Most of the time we live far below the level of which we are capable. There is a tremendous untapped potential within each one of us. For Maslow, achieving that potential involves transcending the merely human. Such sentiments are reminiscent of the esoteric writer George Gurdjieff who dismissed most human beings as sleep walkers – in order to become fully human we must awaken from the slumber within which we conduct our daily lives. Maslow sometimes refers to *metahumans* 'in order to stress that [our] becoming very high or divine or godlike is part of human nature even though it is not often seen in fact'.[19]

By asserting the unlimited nature of human potential Maslow has in effect deified humankind. We are no longer animals driven by the sexual forces of Freudian analysis or the social conditioning of behaviourism. We are slumbering gods.

(c) The Human Potential Movement

Maslow's development of a humanistic psychology was a crucial step in the emergence of the Human Potential Movement. This is a loose coalition of therapies and psychospiritual disciplines which share the goal of helping people achieve their full potential. The futurologist Alvin Toffler has described it in rather acid terms as the 'odds and ends of psychoanalysis, Eastern religion, sexual experimentation, game playing, and old-time revivalism'.[20]

A key player in the growth of the Human Potential Movement was the Esalen Institute founded by Michael Murphy and

Richard Price in Big Sur, California, in 1962. The Institute was inspired by a conversation between the founders and Aldous Huxley. In the years that followed its foundation many of the leaders of the Human Potential Movement were to find a platform for their beliefs and techniques at Esalen. Abraham Maslow himself was a speaker there. Other distinguished guests have included Fritz Perls (the founder of Gestalt therapy), Joseph Campbell (the mythologist), Aldous Huxley, R. D. Laing, Carl Rogers, Paul Tillich, Arnold Toynbee, and Alan Watts, together with a veritable *Who's Who* of leading New Agers.

4. THE POTENTIAL BUSINESS

The Human Potential Movement has resulted in a proliferation of organizations which specialize in self-development seminars and training courses. These vary enormously in style and content. Many of them are theologically neutral and possibly helpful to participants. However, some have achieved notoriety as covert religious organizations. In fact, the term *psycho-cult* is sometimes used to refer to this special category of new religious movement. Some psycho-cults (e.g., scientology) have little connection with the Human Potential Movement beyond their exploitation of the positive image of human potential. Others, such as EST and Silva Mind Control, are more closely related to the movement.

(a) Erhard Seminar Training (EST)

This is probably the most notorious of the self-development courses to have emerged from the Human Potential Movement. EST was created by Werner Erhard (born Jack Rosenberg in 1935), a former car salesman. His own highly eclectic spiritual search took in such diverse practices and faiths as Scientology, Silva Mind Control, Subud, Zen, Gestalt and encounter therapy. Eventually in 1971 he put what he had learned together in his own idiosyncratic synthesis.

Originally EST was highly confrontational. The structure of

seminars was authoritarian with participants being forced to ask permission for such basic necessities as going to the toilet. In a parody of Zen teaching, trainers would insult participants until they achieved enlightenment, or 'got it'.

In the context of EST, enlightenment means undergoing a more or less radical paradigm shift from whatever world-view you possessed before the seminars to Erhard's world-view. Central to that world-view is the belief that we each create and are, therefore, totally responsible for our own reality. This is a widespread assumption amongst New Agers but EST presents it and its implications in an unusually blunt manner. Those implications include an extreme ethical relativism in which whatever is, is right:

> In actuality, each of us, as the sole creator of our universe, is a God, and because we have created all, everything is as important as everything else. When we're fully in touch with what already is and accept what is as more important than what isn't, then all games are over. There's nothing to do, nowhere to go, everything is perfect.[21]

In spite of widespread criticism of the methods involved, EST rapidly became extremely popular. Amongst the public figures who have graduated from EST courses are John Denver, Yoko Ono, and Carly Simon.

Over the years EST has gradually assumed a less intense approach and this was reflected in a change of name to Forum. The popularity of Erhard's approach is reflected in the emergence of a number of other organizations offering similar weekend seminars. Some of the better known are Exegesis, Insight Training Seminars, Lifespring and Life Training Programme.

(b) Silva Mind Control

José Silva began Silva Mind Control in 1966 as a secular meditation technique but as it has developed it has taken on a number of religious beliefs. Drawing on insights from psychoanalysis and Silva's interest in parapsychology, it is promoted as a technique for gaining conscious control over normally unconscious functions of the psyche.

Silva's techniques are borrowed freely from hypnosis, biofeedback, and yoga. Positive thinking and creative visualization are also used extensively, including the invocation of psychic counsellors. Silva interprets these psychic counsellors in Jungian terms as figments of the archetypal imagination but hints that they may be something more than this.[22]

Underlying Silva's system is a belief that everything is ultimately mind. By learning to control our own mental functions we are effectively taking control of the reality which our minds create. Like EST, Silva Mind Control teaches that we are creators and that we are totally responsible for our lives.

5. FROM PSYCHEDELICS TO PSYCHOTECHNOLOGY

At about the same time as the emergence of humanistic psychology another group of American psychologists began experimenting with the mind-altering effects of psychedelic drugs.

(a) Pioneers of the drug culture

An interest in altered states of consciousness and the drugs which can be used to induce them has been part of the counter culture from its earliest days. That pioneer of contemporary explorations of esoteric spirituality, Aldous Huxley, experimented with psychedelic drugs. Through Esalen, his interest in psychedelics was transmitted to members of the nascent Human Potential Movement.

However, the real pioneers of the drug culture were three psychologists working at Harvard University: Ralph Metzner, Richard Alpert and Timothy Leary. Leary was introduced to psychotropic mushrooms during a holiday in Mexico in 1960. The impact of that experience was to change the direction of his career and influence an entire generation of American youth. Returning to Harvard he studied the effects of these mushrooms aided by Metzner. Later they also experimented with LSD.

Perhaps the most outrageous experiment was one suggested by Walter Pahnke and which later became known as the Good

Friday Experiment. Pahnke insisted that there were parallels between drug induced experiences and mystical experiences. They set out to test this by administering psilocybin in the context of a Good Friday service. Those who were given the drug reported much more intense religious experiences than a control group.

(b) Interpreting the psychedelic experience

The psychedelic experience is without doubt an incredibly powerful experience in search of an interpretation. Pahnke's Good Friday Experiment pointed to the possibility of using religious categories.

Perhaps because of the influence of Aldous Huxley, they took the *Bardo Thodol* (*The Tibetan Book of the Dead*) as their guide. Leary argued that what was presented as advice to the souls of the dying was in fact an esoteric guide to mind-expansion. With this insight they were able to perceive in the *Bardo*'s description of psychic travel through unfamiliar realms of consciousness an account of the psychedelic experience. It is a moot point whether this was exegesis or eisegesis: Metzner later made similar claims for one of Hermann Hesse's novels, *The Journey to the East* and others have said as much about *The Lord of the Rings*!

(c) The search for legal alternatives

The third member of the Harvard triumvirate, Richard Alpert, pursued his search for an interpretation to the foothills of the Himalayas. There, the story goes, he met a holy man who consumed his entire stock of LSD without being affected in any way! Alpert was so impressed by this demonstration of control over the mind that he became the man's disciple. He later returned to the USA where, under the name *Baba Ram Dass*, he became a leading spokesman of the New Age. He had discovered, in yoga and meditation, a powerful alternative to the mind-altering effects of drugs.

While Alpert and many others have found their alternative in Eastern religion, yet others have sought more secular ways of altering their minds. One of the pioneers in this field is John Lilly whose work on sensory deprivation (at times assisted by LSD) led to the development of the isolation tank as a tool for achieving altered states of consciousness. Out of that research has grown the present flotation tank business – many New Age centres now offer flotation tanks as a form of relaxation or an aid to mystical experience. Closely related to this is the practice of *rebirthing*. This was developed by a former staff member of EST. Using a hot bath or flotation tank, a womb-like environment is created and the birth trauma is relived.

6. TRANSPERSONAL PSYCHOLOGY

(a) A fourth force

Abraham Maslow took his humanistic psychology a stage further in 1967 when he called for the development of a fourth force in psychology: a school of psychology dedicated to transforming human life. The name *transpersonal* psychology was first suggested by the Czech psychiatrist Stanislav Grof. However, it was quickly adopted by Maslow because, 'The more I think of it, the more this word says what we are all trying to say, that is, beyond individuality, beyond the development of the individual person into something which is more inclusive than the individual person, or which is bigger than he is'.[23]

(b) Psychosynthesis

In fact such a psychology had already been developed by the Italian psychoanalyst, Roberto Assagioli. It was called *psychosynthesis* and is now regarded as the dominant form of transpersonal psychology.

Assagioli had been an orthodox Freudian but rejected the determinism of Freud's approach. Like Maslow his aim was the positive one of enabling people to participate fully and consciously in their personal evolution. He believed that most of us repress our higher selves with the result that we are only half-alive – we are sleep walkers (an idea which Assagioli derived from the esoteric philosophy of Gurdjieff and Ouspensky).

Psychosynthesis is an open-ended system, designed to enable participants to find their own pathway to their higher self (which is a reflection of divine reality). There is no body of literature. Assagioli felt it was important to allow therapists to experiment with and modify the system. In fact, there is no need for the therapist: the process of psychosynthesis may be self-guided.

(c) Beyond psychology

Such an open framework and such an ambitious goal must soon take people past the boundaries of psychology in any meaningful sense of the word. In their quest for pathways to the higher self, transpersonal psychologists have ransacked the world's religions. Old rituals have been revived and new ones devised. Shamanism, Kabbalism, alchemy, witchcraft, divination, the search for the Holy Grail; all these and more have been appropriated in this quest for the transpersonal.

3

Transforming the Spirit

1. EXPLORING MYSTICAL EXPERIENCE

Inspired by the experiments of depth psychology and experiences of alternative states of consciousness, more and more people in the West are turning to the mystical texts of the world's religions for inspiration and guidance. The New Age phenomenon is rehabilitating mysticism for our technological society.

(a) What is mysticism?

The many possible meanings of 'mysticism' create a problem for attempts to discuss it. It is applied to a very wide range of spiritual experiences, spanning the entire range of world religions. This difficulty is compounded by a tendency to use 'mysticism' as a term of abuse. Nineteenth-century Protestant theology stressed ethics and played down experience to such an extent that mysticism was regarded as incompatible with Christianity. This tendency is still sufficiently widespread for New Agers to accuse the churches of an arid dogmatism which leaves no room for inner experience.

Early Christianity adopted the term (from the Graeco-Roman mystery religions) to refer to aspects of the faith which were only accessible to those who had been baptized. Mysticism came to mean experiential knowledge of the central mysteries of the faith. These were mediated to the believer by participation in the sacraments, listening to (or reading) Scripture, and later through signs and images. To this day Eastern Orthodoxy refers to systematic theology as 'mystical theology', arguing that:

> Far from being mutually opposed, theology and mysticism support and complete each other. One is impossible without the other. If *the mystical experience is a personal working out of the content of the common faith*, theology is an expression, for the profit of all, of that which can be experienced by everyone.[1]

Christianity opened up mystical experience to every believer. By contrast, classical mysticism saw it as an experience for a spiritual-intellectual élite. They held out the promise of a direct unmediated experience of ultimate reality. Neoplatonism saw its élite as spearheading the return of created reality to divine unity. Gnosticism was even more élitist, its initiates were agents of the reconstruction of the divine, elements of divinity trapped in matter; by recognizing their own divinity they could assist the divine (and hence themselves) to escape from this world. Both views have presented a recurring temptation to the spiritualizing tendencies within Christianity. They have been kept alive by the western occult tradition and their interaction with Christianity has, over the centuries, generated a number of heresies. Some New Agers look to these traditions for their understanding of mysticism. But most accept the very broad view which is popular today: 'mystical' and 'spiritual' have become almost interchangeable terms.

An alternative approach is to treat mysticism empirically, focussing on the recurring features in reports of mystical experience. Such features include a sense of presence; joy or well-being; altered experiences of time and space; union with transcendent reality; and union with nature. The difficulty is that this approach tends to assume that different experiences are, in fact, the same. This is in keeping with the widespread belief that all religions are merely alternative interpretations imposed upon a common core of human experiences. It can overlook the fact that mystical union can refer to an experience of personal relationship with God (in Christianity), the total loss of self (in Buddhism), or identification with the Absolute (in some forms of Hinduism).

(b) The turn to the East

Since the Enlightenment western culture has played down spiritual experience. Thus many men and women in search of the spirit have turned to the other great cultures which have become increasingly accessible during the same period. African cultures were overlooked as primitive. Islamic culture was relatively inaccessible. The eighteenth and nineteenth centuries were the ages in which the Imperial powers of Northern Europe turned their attention to the East.

One aspect of this turn to the East was a philosophical reaction against the Enlightenment's overemphasis on human reason. The seminal figure of this movement was Arthur Schopenhauer (1788–1860). His synthesis of German Idealism and Hindu metaphysics was an inspiration to Friedrich Nietzche (whose myth of the Superman was to become notorious in the debased form adopted by Nazism), Carl Jung, and the Nobel-prizewinning novelist Hermann Hesse. As you might expect the influence of this movement on Jung and Hesse is one of the roots of the widespread interest in eastern thought which emerged during the 1950s and 1960s.

If the mythology of western occultism is to be believed, there was already a long history of association between the occult underground of western culture and eastern religions. Many legends associate the Knights Templar with esoteric spiritual traditions (purportedly learned from Muslim mystics). Another link between West and East is discerned in the sexual magic of western occultism which is often traced back to Tantric Yoga. Whether or not there is any truth in the legends, nineteenth-century occultists certainly displayed considerable interest in the East. The most prominent force behind the occult interest in eastern philosophy was the Theosophical Society (founded in 1875 by a Russian emigrée, Helena Petrovna Blavatsky). In spite of numerous defections and the formation of several splinter groups, theosophy survived to become one of the factors in the twentieth-century revival of Hinduism and a major force within the New Age movement.

(c) Meditation

The westerners who went east in search of drug free Enlightenment brought back with them meditation. This word is almost as difficult to use as 'mysticism' and for much the same reasons. It is a blanket term applied to a wide range of psychological and spiritual disciplines found in all the major religious traditions including Christianity.

New Agers, like many other westerners, assume that experience is prior to interpretation. This is implicit in the popular misunderstanding of the scientific method: we make observations (which, if accurate, may be given the accolade of 'fact') and then use our reason to deduce theories (which, because they depend on our fallible minds, must be less reliable than the facts behind them). Applied to religion, this becomes: religious experience comes before theology and philosophy. Therefore you cannot argue with the experience. This easily becomes a spiritual pragmatism in which any technique that produces an experience is regarded as valid.

This approach is alien to most of the traditions from which New Agers draw. In both Zen and Yoga the meditation exercises have been carefully developed to generate particular alternative states of consciousness which reinforce the relevant philosophical perspective. The same could be said of Christian meditation: here the meditative techniques, properly understood, are not seen as achieving anything in themselves. Rather their disciplined practice is symbolic of a personal commitment to be open to God's activity. The key note of Christians as diverse as Julian of Norwich, Hildegarde of Bingen, St John of the Cross and John Bunyan is grace rather than works.

Many meditative techniques are used by New Agers. Some look to Japanese and Chinese traditions, e.g., Zen Buddhism or the dynamic physical meditation of the martial arts. More recently there has been increasing interest in occult forms of meditation such as shamanism and pathworking. However the dominant form of meditation used by New Agers is Yoga.

(d) Yoga

The word *Yoga* comes from a Sanskrit verb meaning 'to untie' (it shares a common linguistic origin with the English word 'yoke'). It refers to the union of the individual mind with ultimate reality.

The precise nature of the ultimate reality in question depends on the form of Hinduism. Different branches of Hinduism have used Yoga for achieving union with ultimate realities as diverse as the True Self, an impersonal Absolute, and personal deity. But, whatever the goal, it is clear, both from its etymology and its traditional use, that Yoga is a spiritual discipline.

In common usage, the word denotes a carefully developed set of physical, psychological, and spiritual techniques all intended to bring about this union. But 'Yoga' also refers to the underlying philosophy. This was systematized by the Hindu scholar Patanjali. When he lived is not certain: scholars date his *Yoga Sutras* between the second century BC and the fourth century AD. However, his contribution to Indian spirituality is clear enough. He took 'an enormous and self-contradictory range of ideas, practices, taboos, and beliefs'[2] dating back perhaps 5000 years and moulded it into a coherent system of belief and practice.

In Patanjali's system there are eight basic stages in one's spiritual progress to union, Enlightenment or salvation. The first steps, and the foundation for everything else, are basic rules of diet and hygiene. While some of these rules coincide with western ideas it must be borne in mind that their purpose was not physical well-being but spiritual.

Next comes *Hatha Yoga*. This is the system of physical exercises (*asanas*) which most westerners identify with the word Yoga. *Hatha* (pronounced 'hut-ha') is a composite of the Sanskrit words for sun and moon, referring to the body's consumption and acquisition of vital energy. In addition to the postures, a complex system of breathing exercises (*pranayama*) is taught. By learning to control the physical breath, the student of Yoga is also bringing the psychic energy associated with the breath (*prana*) under control. This in turn contributes to bringing the psychic energy associated with the body (*kundalini*) under control.

Once these fundamentals are learned the student is ready to commence the exercises in concentration and meditation which lead ultimately to union.

Yoga has been practised in the West for over a century. The first books on the subject were published by the Theosophical Society. However, it is the succession of Hindu missions to the western world that have been mainly responsible for its increasing popularity. The first of these began with the arrival of Swami Vivekananda. He founded the Vedanta Societies and wrote extensively on various forms of Yoga including *Karma Yoga* (the Yoga of physical activity and work), *Bhakti Yoga* (the Yoga of devotion to particular Hindu deities), *Jnana Yoga* (the Yoga of analysis or spiritual discrimination), and *Raja Yoga* (the system of meditation exercises for which Hatha Yoga is the foundation).

Yet another form of Yoga has been popularized by the Maharishi Mahesh Yogi (with his Transcendental Meditation) and the International Society for Krishna Consciousness (usually known as ISKCON or the Hare Krishna Movement). Both promote a simple form of Bhakti Yoga (religious devotion) known as *Japa Yoga*. In Japa Yoga a word of power or *mantra* is said repeatedly. Since the word is often the name of Hindu deity its repetition is an act of religious devotion as well as an exercise in concentration.

Western occultism has taken a particular interest in *Tantric Yoga*. This might be described as the 'quick and dirty' path to Enlightenment. More orthodox forms of Yoga rely on years of ascetic discipline to overcome habit, raise *Kundalini* and achieve Enlightenment. *Tantrism* deliberately flouts the taboos of orthodox Hinduism in order to achieve more rapid progress. Thus followers of this path will indulge in five means which are normally forbidden: *madya* (wine), *mansa* (flesh), *matsya* (fish), *mudra* (parched grain), and *maithuna* (sexual intercourse). These are believed to give rapid access to large amounts of spiritual energy. The sexual practices of Tantrism have been of particular interest to westerners. They were integrated into modern ritual magic by Aleister Crowley who was a major influence on L. Ron Hubbard (the founder of Scientology).

A common question is whether Yoga can be limited to physical exercise. Some authorities argue that it can. For example, Prabhu Guptara argues that Yoga originated as an atheistic reaction against Indian temple worship and that, in practice, millions of Yoga students worldwide do it without any interest in its possible psychological or spiritual dimensions. On the other hand, B. K. S. Iyengar, one of the foremost teachers of Hatha Yoga, reacts angrily to the suggestion that it can be merely a form of physical exercise. For him it is inherently religious. Carl Jung makes a similar point in his investigations of Yoga: 'Yoga practice is unthinkable, and would also be ineffectual, without the ideas on which it is based. It works the physical and the spiritual into one another in an extraordinarily complete way'.[3] As a former Yoga teacher pointed out to me, Yoga shorn of its spiritual dimension is no longer Yoga – it is only physical exercise.

2. THE REVIVAL OF OCCULTISM

Another dimension of New Age spirituality is the input from western occultism. While some people were turning to the East others were looking to the past for alternative spiritualities. The result has been a dramatic revival in the fortunes of western occultism. It is striking that this has occurred during a period of unprecedented scientific and technological progress. Even more striking is the result of a 1985 survey of American Neo-Pagans which revealed that 'roughly 16% were either programmers, technical writers, or scientists.'[4]

The mood of the times clearly had something to do with the reappearance of occultism. There had already been a major philosophical and artistic reaction to the arid rationalism of the Enlightenment. Romanticism in Europe and Transcendentalism in the United States both encouraged people to explore the spiritual dimension of their nature. Closely related to this was a strong sentimental attachment to the past.

Amongst those who harked back to past spiritual glories

were a number of Freemasons who felt that it had degenerated. Drawing on the esoteric history of the society and embellishing it with ideas drawn from their own reading of mediaeval history, they laid the foundation for a number of societies dedicated to the revival of ceremonial magic.

The most important of these was the *Hermetic Order of the Golden Dawn*. Founded by an eccentric Francophile Scot, MacGregor Mathers, it rapidly caught the imagination of a number of influential figures. In part this was due to the radical aristocratic politics of its founder (who was dedicated to the restoration of the Stuarts to the British throne and was sympathetic to Irish nationalism). Its most important member was the poet and Irish nationalist, W. B. Yeats. However, it also had a number of Christian adherents including Evelyn Underhill and Charles Williams (there was even an offshoot of Golden Dawn run by Anglo-Catholic priests!).

Another member of Golden Dawn was to become notorious as 'the wickedest man in the world'. After an unsuccessful bid for the leadership of the Order at the turn of this century, Aleister Crowley left to become the leader of the English branch of Golden Dawn's German counterpart, the *Ordo Templi Orientis*. Like Golden Dawn, OTO was involved in radical politics, offering a meeting place for men who in later years were influential in the development of Nazism. These connections allowed Crowley to offer his services to the British Secret Service in the 1930s. This, in turn, brought him into contact with Dennis Wheatley (who derived much of his knowledge of ceremonial magic from Crowley).

The revival of witchcraft is a more recent phenomenon than that of ceremonial magic. Most authorities point to Margaret Murray's 1924 *Encyclopaedia Britannica* article on the subject as the seminal work. She created the myth of an underground pre-Christian pagan religion. This, in turn, inspired people such as Gerald Gardner and Alex Sanders to develop living covens and appropriate rituals. From their example and writing have sprung the two main forms of modern witchcraft: Gardnerian and Alexandrian. However, the individualism and creativity amongst witches is so great that there are probably as many forms of witchcraft as there are active covens.

3. DIVINATION IN THE NEW AGE

Divination is usually understood as the use of supernatural means to foretell the future or discover what is hidden. By extension, the discovery of what is hidden may be taken to include gaining access to inner wisdom.

Over the centuries many techniques have been used in divination. The augurs of classical Mediterranean culture would read the flight of birds or the internal organs of sacrificial animals.

An important class of divinatory techniques are the *mantic* techniques. These include *geomancy* (in which the reading is based on patterns of thrown earth or random dots produced by the diviner while in a trance state), *cheiromancy* (the reading of patterns on the hand), *tea leaf reading*, and *I Ching* (the Taoist system in which throws of yarrow sticks or coins direct you to particular passages in a book of oracles). The common factor in all these is the drawing of a message from a very complex (and apparently random) pattern. Also related to this approach would be the reading of playing cards (especially *Tarot* cards).

But most important of all the forms of divination is undoubtedly astrology.

(a) Astrology

(i) *The history of astrology*: The origin of western astrology is shrouded in mystery. Astrologers often claim that it can be traced back to Mesopotamia in the second millenium BC. It is true that archaeological evidence of astronomical observations have been found dating from that period or even earlier. But historical evidence for astrology only appears at a much later date, e.g., Herodotus (writing in the fifth century BC) comments on Egyptian interest in astrology. The signs of the Zodiac were already well established by the time of Herodotus. However, astro-archaeological investigation of their origin points not to Mesopotamia but to the Phoenician or Minoan empires. It is arguable that their original function (and, indeed, that of the classical constellations as a whole) was navigational.

Apparently astrology played a vital role in the state religion of the Neo-Babylonian Empire from the seventh century BC. Its overthrow by Cyrus in 536 BC led to the dispersal of professional astrologers throughout the Near East.

An important step forward came with the codification of astrology by the Greek Egyptian astronomer Ptolemy in the second century AD. By that time astrology was widespread throughout the Graeco-Roman world. And so matters continued in spite of the rise of Christendom.

Strictly speaking astrology was not esoteric or occult knowledge. Those terms denote bodies of knowledge accessible only to a small élite carefully controlled by elaborate initiation processes. By contrast astrology was an integral part of western thought up to and after the Reformation. The English historian Keith Thomas comments that

> At the beginning of the sixteenth century astrological doctrines were part of the educated man's picture of the universe and its workings. . . . Astrology was . . . less a separate discipline than an aspect of a generally accepted world picture. . . . It was not a coterie doctrine, but an essential aspect of the intellectual framework in which men were educated.[5]

(ii) *Classical astrology*: The basic assumptions underlying astrology are fairly straightforward. For classical astronomers the most striking feature of the heavens was the regularity of celestial motion in contrast to the irregularity of life on earth. They assumed that celestial bodies were superior to the creatures of the sub-lunary or terrestrial sphere. By extension they believed that these superior bodies ruled over their terrestrial inferiors, influencing this world in a variety of ways.

The limitations of astronomical observations prior to the invention of the telescope led them to postulate a single system of seven planets moving relative to the earth and each other in a well-defined region of the sky – the plane of the ecliptic. The twelve constellations which form the background to the ecliptic constitute the zodiac, the fixed frame of reference against which the movement of the planets is measured. The precise nature of the heavenly influence at any time could be determined by drawing up a horoscope.

There were four main branches of classical astrology:

General predictions sought insight into the big issues of the day from knowledge of the future movements of the planets, impending eclipses, conjunctions, etc. For example, one of the political power-brokers of the Tudor court, Cardinal Wolsey, timed the departure of an embassy to France in 1527 to coincide with an astrologically propitious moment.

Nativities or birth charts provided general information about an individual's prospects in life. They could also provide more specific information (e.g., by casting *annual revolutions* focussing specifically on the coming year).

Elections used astrology to choose the right moment for some action. By comparing the client's birth chart with what is known of future planetary movements the astrologer would identify the most propitious times for going on a journey, getting married, or even something more routine like having a haircut or a bath.

Horary questions were introduced by Arab astronomers. They believed that the astrologer could answer any question by casting a horoscope for the moment at which the question was asked. I have already mentioned the medical application but any personal problem could be stated in the form of a horary question and appropriate astrological advice received.

The basic principles of astrology are straightforward but the actual practice of casting a horoscope is a complicated and intellectually demanding task, involving large numbers of sophisticated astronomical calculations. Given the lack of precision in time measurement for most of the history of astrology and the scope for error in the calculations, there was room for considerable variation. But, on top of that, the whole issue of interpretation introduces a subjective dimension to astrology. Recognizing that we are not isolated individuals the astrologer might feel that it is necessary to compare our horoscope with that of our wife, or parents, or friends. The qualities of the planets were handed down in mythological form – and these mythologies were not always consistent. Deciding which variables were significant in a particular case and how to interpret them was definitely an art rather than a science.

(iii) *The social role of classical astrology*: What made this extremely complicated art so popular? What part did it play in mediaeval society?

It was an integral part of the mediaeval world-view. You might say it played a mediating role between metaphysics and everyday life. It was built upon the basic assumptions of the Aristotelian philosophy which dominated western culture. But it offered practical answers to everyday questions. Without astrology many of the significant events of life (particularly the misfortunes) would have remained inexplicable, meaningless absurdities.

It satisfied the very human desire for explanations. This extended to sheer intellectual curiosity. Early psychologies were built upon astrology: we still speak of people being jovial, mercurial, or saturnine. Astrology was also the basis of the earliest attempts to achieve a scientific explanation of historical and political events. Thus the English Reformation was put down to a conjunction of Mars, Mercury, and Jupiter in Aries in 1553. Even the great physicist Isaac Newton thought that he could use astrological data to reconstruct ancient history.

But, for many people, the most important role of the astrologer was as personal counsellor. A visit to the astrologer has been likened to the mediaeval equivalent of a visit to the psychoanalyst. We often think of astrology as fatalistic, as teaching that our lives are held in the iron grip of the stars. In fact that was never the case with the more respectable practitioners. On the contrary, the whole point was that by offering clients some idea of the possibilities they might choose the better possibilities.

So astrology offered knowledge: self-knowledge and knowledge of current affairs. But, as Francis Bacon pointed out during the hey-day of astrology, 'Knowledge is power.' The dividing line between divination and magical manipulation of reality is subtle at the best of times. In fact, astrologers often crossed the line. In offering explanations they were holding out the prospect of control. Astrological advice could be used to manipulate events and astrological imagery and correspondences often found their way into ritual magic.

Given its close connection with Aristotelianism, it is hardly surprising that interest in astrology collapsed at the Enlightenment. What is surprising is that so many of those who were instrumental in ushering in modern science should have clung to astrology for so long while attacking the philosophical foundations on which it was built. It became one of the first casualties of secularization.

(iv) *Astrology in the New Age*: Astrology was driven underground by the Enlightenment but its long and varied history bears witness to its incredible capacity to adapt to new social situations.

In the nineteenth century the Theosophical Society adopted astrology and this added considerably to its popularity. At about the same time a number of astrologers began arguing that astrology could be explained in scientific terms: the discipline was beginning to adapt to the new cultural situation.

An interest in the scientific verifiability of astrology is a recurring feature today. I have already mentioned Carl Jung's experiments. But perhaps the best known and most respected investigation was that undertaken by Michel Gauquelin. He has discovered statistically significant correlations between birth charts and choice of profession. So disturbing was his research that the Committee for the Scientific Investigation of Claims of the Paranormal (CSICOP) published fraudulent data in an attempt to discredit it! The impression that astrology is scientific is further enhanced by the widespread use of computers to cast horoscopes.

But what really helped astrology adapt to modern culture was the emergence of psychoanalysis. Even before Jung's experiments astrologers were becoming aware of the potential of psychology. As early as 1924 the Theosophical Society was publishing material on psychological astrology.

Psychology is better able to explain the phenomenon of astrology than, say, astronomy. Although astronomical phenomena such as the sunspot cycle do have an observable effect on the earth's climate and magnetic field, the influence of the planets can only be marginal. One psychological interpretation is that astrology offers a convenient symbolic system by which we can project the hidden structure of the collective unconscious. In this way astrology becomes a tool for greater self-understanding and offers a map for personal development. What traditional astrology saw as tragic flaws revealed by the birth chart, this interpretation views as weakness in personality structure, opportunities for learning and growth.

This may sound new and it certainly fits in to our cultural situation. But it is as old as magic itself. The horoscope has become a kind of psycho-cosmogram: a device by which we can pursue the route to self-actualization. A very similar path had already been taken by the Gnostics who developed elaborate cosmic myths which functioned as symbol systems detailing the path of spiritual growth.

(b) Tarot

The Tarot are a pack of special playing cards widely used in divination. Their origins are obscure and they may, in fact, be an amalgam of two different types of card. A traditional Tarot pack can certainly be divided into two distinct parts.

The twenty-two Major cards are the familiar ones bearing images such as the hanged man, and the fool. It is often suggested that these representations may bear some relation to the deities of the Hellenistic mystery religions.

There are also fifty-six Minor cards arranged in four suits: Wands, Cups, Swords, and Coins. These were the forerunners of modern playing cards, the Tarot suits having evolved into Clubs, Hearts, Spades, and Diamonds respectively. One theory is that these suits correspond to the Four Treasures of the *Tuatha de Danaan* in Irish mythology. Alternatively, they may reflect the four major segments of mediaeval society (Swords: the nobility, Cups (or chalices): the clergy, Coins: the merchants, and Wands: the peasants).

(i) *The history of Tarot*: It is often suggested that their use as a form of divination is ancient. However, they do not appear to have formed an important part of the diviner's arsenal in Mediaeval England.[6] Their occult use was popularized by a seventeenth-century French Protestant minister, Antoine de

Gebelin. His writings on the subject influenced the great French occultist Eliphas Levi and through him they became an established part of French occultism. Perhaps because of MacGregor Mathers' love for France, this French tradition was adopted by Golden Dawn. Members were expected to produce their own Tarot pack as one of the stages of initiation. Two designs which are widely used today (the Waite Tarot and the Crowley Tarot) originated in this process.

(ii) *Using the Tarot*: The use of Tarot has developed in two distinct ways. Its popular use as a tool of divination involves laying the entire pack in one or more of a variety of patterns. The location of a card within the pattern affects its significance.

A more important occult use of the Tarot is as an aid to meditation. This approach is associated with the occult tradition of Kabbalism and is traceable to Eliphas Levi. Only the Major cards are used and they are taken to represent various pathways between the ten levels of consciousness recognized by Kabbalism. Understood in this way the cards form the basis for certain visualization exercises (the techniques known as *pathworking*) and for certain rituals.

(iii) *Tarot in the New Age*: Like other forms of divination, they have been given a certain legitimacy by psychoanalysis. It is not uncommon to find the Major Trumps being identified with Jungian archetypes. Thus the Tarot may be used as an aid for diagnosing an individual's state of psychological development or spiritual growth.

4. CHANNELLING

Channelling has become almost an identifying characteristic of the New Age phenomenon, on a par with crystals. It has been popularized by the actress Shirley MacLaine, for whom encounters with channellers were significant stages in her spiritual pilgrimage.

Channelling is the process of gaining access to information (or spiritual wisdom) from a source other than your ordinary consciousness. The phenomenon is very similar to that of classical spirit mediumship. However the negative image of mediumship has led to the adoption of a new name. The term comes from UFOlogy, where it was used to describe telepathic contact with extra-terrestrials.

Most New Age channels claim to be in contact with some external entity. Some believe they are in contact with extra-terrestrials. Others claim to channel dolphins. Uri Geller claims to be in contact with a super-computer located in the future. Many make spiritual claims: they are in contact with Jesus, ascended spiritual masters (e.g., Ramtha, a 35,000 year old warrior priest), discarnate spirits, or simply God. A minority claim that they are accessing their own unconscious or higher self.

Some degree of trance state is common. When the channel enters this state, his or her contact may communicate by auto-matic writing or, more usually, through the vocal chords of the channel. The most dramatic cases may involve a radical change in personality, mannerisms, and even physical appearance.

(a) Gospels for the New Age

Channelling or mediumship has been the basis for many apocry-phal gospels and volumes of spiritual wisdom during the last century. Amongst the best known examples are *The Aquarian Gospel of Jesus the Christ* (transcribed by Levi Dowling from the Akashic records at the turn of the century); *The Book of Urantia; A Course in Miracles* (based on voices heard by Helen Schucman and one of which she identified as Jesus); and the *Books of Seth*.

The messages are diverse but they generally reinforce the New Age world-view. A common feature is the proclamation that we are on the threshold of a New Age – an age in which spirituality will be rediscovered and humanity will live in har-mony with nature. At the same time there are often warnings of cataclysmic events which will usher in this New Age – a 'cleansing' which will eliminate those who are unfit to benefit from this new dispensation. Advice on how to prepare for the New Age abounds. Other common features include the belief that we create our own reality (and are therefore totally responsible for all that happens to us) and that we are capable of self-perfection.

(b) Interpreting channelling

Broadly speaking interpretations of this phenomenon fall into three categories.

The secular interpretation: Secular humanism as represented by such pressure groups as CSICOP has a clear and straightforward explanation. For them, channels like spirit mediums are frauds. The fact that large amounts of money are involved (a private session with a well-known channel can cost hundreds of pounds per hour) merely strengthens their conviction that fraud is behind it.

Psychological interpretations: Channelling may be a form of voluntary or involuntary access to parts of the unconscious mind.

Some of the more bizarre cases of channelling may be accounted for in terms of *multiple personality disorder*. Victims of this disorder undergo dramatic changes of personality; their voices may change; and so may their appearance as they take on entirely different sets of mannerisms, ways of walking, etc. Often MPD is associated with serious childhood trauma such as might be caused by sexual abuse. This interpretation is supported by a reported correlation of channelling with the kinds of childhood trauma that lead to MPD.

Literal interpretations: New Agers who regard channelling as a genuine form of communication with external entities tend to talk in terms of 'voluntary possession'. A similar interpretation would commend itself to many evangelical Christians. The evangelical interpretation would depart from the literal New Age explanation at two points:

(a) Is the phenomenon truly voluntary? Many channels seem to be able to turn this gift on and off at will. However, they may not have actively sought the gift in the first place. There are parallels with even more extreme situations such as the case of Sathya Sai Baba (in which the boy's personality appears to have been completely and permanently displaced by a personality claiming to be a deceased Hindu holy man).

(b) Are the entities involved beneficient? Are they spiritual masters seeking to enlighten us or demonic forces seeking to delude us? Like much modern psychoanalysis, the channelling phenomenon relies on the naive assumption that everything which emerges from the psyche or 'higher spiritual planes' must be good.

5. NATURAL MAGIC

The popular classification of magic[7] into 'black' and 'white' does not sit easily with the occult understanding of good and evil. Occultists treat good and evil as polar rather than absolute opposites. Far from being mutually exclusive they are mutually dependent. Rather than speaking of good and evil, they may talk in terms of positive and negative or creative and destructive. A balance needs to be maintained. Ultimately the harmony of the cosmos depends on maintaining a balance between the creative and destructive cycles of existence. For the sake of harmony an occultist is unlikely to restrict him or herself exclusively to 'white' or 'creative' practices.

A more common classification amongst practitioners would be 'natural' and 'ceremonial'. Natural magic entails the occult employment of natural forces for spiritual (or material) ends. An important aspect of modern natural magic is the development of power-from-within: the actualization of one's own psychic powers through techniques such as positive thinking and visualization. But natural magic also involves much herbal lore. The employment of crystal power would be yet another example of natural magic.

Ceremonial magic is the kind which features strongly in the novels of Dennis Wheatley. It is characterized by more or less elaborate ritual and the extensive use of symbols. The purpose of this activity is the invocation of spirit entities, or pagan deities, or archetypes (depending on the interpretation).

(a) Creative visualization

The single most important technique in modern occultism is creative visualization. Entire courses in natural and ceremonial magic have built upon this foundation.[8]

In its broadest form, the term visualization denotes the use of mental imagery to achieve desired ends. Such techniques are widespread amongst New Agers but two uses in particular stand out. One of these is the therapeutic use already described in Chapter 1. The other is *prosperity consciousness*. If using visualization to create a positive attitude can bring about changes in our physical body, it can do the same for our larger environment. Thus you are invited to imagine particular social or economic objectives. Successful visualization equips you to realize the desired objective.

Clearly visualization is more than mere day-dreaming or wishing. In fact, harbouring the sentiment that your visualizations are only dreams is a sure way of preventing the achievement of your objectives. The act of visualization is more an act of will – it is active imagination.

Visualization uses the power of our imagination to bring about changes in physical reality; either our own bodies or the world around us. The explanation is that it changes the world by changing our attitude so that we are better able to go out and get what we want. We all do this to some extent: we go into that race determined to win, into that exam determined to pass, into that meeting determined to get the outcome we desire. Imagination is being harnessed as a motivating force for human behaviour (an idea as old as Aristotle).

But there is another aspect to visualization which emerges as soon as we accept the fundamental occult law of correspondence, 'As above, so below, but in a different form.' What this means is that the macrocosm (the universe and/or God depending on the cosmology of the occultist) and the microcosm (the human being either as a whole or his or her inner self) are intimately connected. Every spiritual reality has this-worldly counterparts.

If you know what symbols correspond to the spiritual reality you wish to invoke, you can force its manifestation by collecting those symbols together in an appropriate fashion. The symbols of ritual magic affect the macrocosm through their effect on the microcosm of the magician. It is a fundamental principle of western magic that by changing our inner world we can coerce the macrocosm into corresponding changes.

Occult visualization simply does away with the external ritual. It internalizes the symbols. Constructing a mental image is regarded as tantamount to creating the spiritual reality, forcing it to manifest on the physical level. Thus Melita Denning writes,

> Truly, *by the power of this source channelled through the conscious and unconscious levels of your own psyche*, the action takes places on the corresponding levels of the external universe, to bring about the presentation to you on the earthly level of what you have imaged. *That is WHY you can truly affirm that what you visualize IS YOURS NOW.* Astrally it is YOURS; mentally and spiritually it is YOURS, because you are activating those levels by means of your own mental and spiritual forces so that what you create astrally shall be REALIZED materially.[9]

It comes as no surprise to find that visualization and similar imagination developing exercises form a fundamental part of any textbook on natural magic. If you like, the mental images created by the occultist constitute the symbols for an internalized symbolic magic.

Some magical systems have converted visualization into a systematic graded spiritual discipline. The author of one such system comments that,

> What begins with the exercise of the controlled creation of a one-dimensional image becomes the creation of a three-dimensional image, then the transmutation of a concept or idea into an image, then in turn to the activation of people and things and people and the creation of situations that eventually transpire in the realm we call the 'physical'.[10]

But this is still low magic, tinkering with our environment. High magic takes us inwards and here too imaginative techniques akin to visualization are used. Through the power of imagination practitioners claim to be able to enter the inner realms – the place of the gods and the place of the dead. Imagination has been used in an analogous way to the invocation of ritual magic.

Occult visualization in both its low and high forms is widely practised in New Age and related circles (e.g., in EST and Silva Mind Control). Another, still more secular form would be the positive thinking of Mind Dynamics.

(b) Shamanism

This term derives from the primitive culture of Siberia but has been extended by anthropology and comparative religion to refer to a set of related practices found in many cultures. In this broad sense, the shaman acts as a go-between with the spirit world on behalf of the community. As such he or she may be called upon to work as a spiritual director (the task may well include that of guiding members of the community through their rites of passage), a healer, or a psychopomp (one who guides the souls of the recently departed to their eternal resting place). Typically the shaman operates in a trance state which may have been induced by the use of psychedelic drugs.

Although their veracity has been called into question, the works of Carlos Castaneda offer a very clear picture of a shaman in the person of Don Juan. More than any other these books have been responsible for introducing the concept of the shaman to New Agers. Today shamanism is widely regarded by New Agers as a useful psychotechnology (often amalgamated with transpersonal psychology).

Transforming the World:
The New Age and Society

1. THE TRANSFORMATION OF POLITICS

Many New Agers look for a transformation in politics. Marilyn Ferguson asserts that 'Eventually, anyone concerned with the transformation of the individual must engage in social action'.[1] She claims that traditional politics robs individuals of their sense of social responsibility. Its hierarchical structure is seen as a fundamental stumbling block to the achievement of many of the larger goals of the New Age.

But these social and political structures are deeply ingrained. More recently, they have proved themselves an attractive alternative to Marxism in Eastern Europe. How are such firmly established structures to be displaced by New Age alternatives?

(a) The hundredth monkey effect

The mechanism to which New Agers usually appeal is that of critical mass or *the hundredth monkey effect*. Critical mass is a concept from nuclear physics: in any sample of fissile material (e.g., plutonium) large unstable atoms are continually breaking down, releasing energetic particles (and gamma radiation). Some of these particles escape from the material or are absorbed by stable atoms. Others collide with further unstable atoms and the process is repeated, producing a chain reaction. If a sufficient mass of fissile material is concentrated in one place the rate at which energetic particles produce further atomic fission outweighs the rate at which they are absorbed or escape. The result is a catastrophic cascade of fission, an atomic explosion.

In 1979 Lyall Watson related an anecdotal account of analogous behaviour amongst groups of Japanese monkeys. Apparently some of them had begun washing potatoes in the sea and this behaviour was gradually being learned by other monkeys. However, according to Watson,

> In the autumn of that year [1958] an unspecified number of monkeys on Koshima were washing sweet potatoes in the sea . . . Let us say, for argument's sake, that the number was ninety-nine and that at eleven o'clock on a Tuesday morning, one further convert was added to the fold in the usual way. But the addition of the hundredth monkey apparently carried the number across some sort of threshold, pushing it through a kind of critical mass, because by that evening almost everyone was doing it. Not only that, but the habit seems to have jumped natural barriers and to have appeared spontaneously . . . in colonies on other islands and on the mainland.[2]

This story was picked up and applied to the New Age by Ken Keyes. More than a million copies of his book, *The Hundredth Monkey*, have been printed since its publication in 1982. But the idea of critical mass as the mechanism for political transformation was already an integral part of New Age politics. In 1979, Mark Satin (then a major New Age political theorist) published a book in which he stated,

> A critical mass is the number of concerned and committed people it would take to move the continent – democratically – in a New Age direction. Estimates on what makes a critical mass range all the way from 2 per cent (Transcendental Meditation) to 20 per cent (Erich Fromm). The implication is that commitment and concern have a certain political weight of their own and that a minority of concerned people can and *should* affect the democratic process more strongly than a larger number of apathetic people.[3]

Thus New Age politics is the politics of the pressure group. But the main focus of political effort is at the individual level.

If Satin and others are correct, the most effective way to bring about political transformation is by concentrating on personal transformation until the critical mass is reached. National and, ultimately, global transformation will then follow spontaneously.

This sounds remarkably similar to the old arguments used by some Christians to justify the priority of personal evangelism over social concern. And it may have the same effect, namely, of relieving the believer of any responsibility to struggle with difficult social and political issues. Such a position does not admit the spiritual power of social and political structures.

(b) Networking and communities

(i) *Networking*: This term from the world of computing is used to describe the practice which has led to the New Age's frustratingly amorphous structure. A network is a loose association of people related to each other by some common interest. The primary form of connection is usually a mailing list or directory. However some networks (such as Alternatives at St James's Church, Piccadilly) rely on regular open meetings at which people can meet with other New Agers.

The most sophisticated networks are built around computer bulletin boards. These permit virtually instantaneous identification of and communication between people with common interests anywhere in the world. However, while some New Agers are enthusiastic about such developments others rightly question the security of such systems. They may actually permit greater central government monitoring of people's private lives.

There is nothing specifically New Age about the concept of a network. On the contrary it may be regarded as the space age equivalent of the old school tie. Such informal and semiformal directories and fora for communication also have a long history within orthodox Christianity. Similarly computer networks are used to great effect by the scientific community to permit more rapid communication of new ideas and discovery and facilitate debate.

The network serves a number of important purposes. It enables people to find the resources they want or make contact with people who have similar interests. A typical British example would be the Holistic Network. It publishes an annual directory of practitioners in a wide range of complementary therapies and personal development techniques. Similarly the membership directory of the Scientific and Medical Network lists more than 700 people (mostly professional scientists and doctors) giving contact addresses and details of research interests.

Networks also allow New Agers to make contact with people outside the movement who share some of its central concerns (e.g., peace, environmentalism, animal rights or mysticism). Thus they enable New Agers to further their interests through cooperation with non-New Age individuals and groups. This often confuses outside observers leading them to take New Age endorsement of an organisation (e.g., Friends of the Earth) as evidence that it is a New Age group. At the same time this aspect of networking creates amongst New Agers a sense of being in the vanguard of a much larger (though still largely unconscious) movement.

(ii) *Communities*: These are the next most important New Age social structures after networks. Communal life is attractive to New Agers because it is a clear alternative to the competitive individualism of western society. It reflects certain principles which New Agers value highly, e.g., interdependence and cooperation. Because of their visibility such communities tend to become focal points of the movement, acting as clearing houses for the latest techniques of personal and social transformation. They may also regard themselves as pilot plants, seeking to demonstrate the viability of New Age socio-political alternatives to the wider society.

(c) The New Age political agenda

In 1979 Mark Satin suggested that a viable 'new politics' was already emerging from the

> feminist, environmental, spiritual, and human potential movements, the appropriate technology, simple living, decentralist, and 'world order' movements . . . out of the

work of a couple of hundred sympathetic economists and spiritual philosophers, businesspeople and workers' self-management people, systems analysts and psychoanalysts, physicists and poets . . . [4]

He is disarmingly frank about the minuteness of the New Age's political power base. But the statement also offers a useful resumé of the kinds of issues which attract New Age attention and political activity.

Global political structures are of particular interest to them. New Agers are unashamed internationalists, giving moral support to the activities of the United Nations Organization. Pressure groups such as Planetary Citizens and World Goodwill exist to provide a New Age spiritual counterpart to such political efforts. The ideological reason behind such support is a widespread belief in the 'planetization' of human society: that we are evolving spiritually and socially towards a single united humanity.

Paradoxically they are also decentralists. They believe that minimal government is the best government and that political responsibility should be devolved from national and international centres to local communities and individuals.

One major issue of concern to New Agers was nuclear disarmament. This is less of an issue now that East and West seem to have achieved some kind of *rapprochement*. While some New Agers participated in conventional peace protests,[5] others have opted for more spiritual ways of influencing the situation. Transcendental Meditation is well known for its claim that crime and violence decline markedly when more than two per cent of a population practise TM regularly. The Lucis Trust (the parent body of World Goodwill) encourages New Agers to meet in meditative groups (Triangles) to make the Great Affirmation, a prayer for peace and planetary cleansing. Many other groups recommend creative visualization and affirmation as ways of influencing society in a more peaceful direction.

As Satin points out, feminism is firmly on the New Age agenda. This is a relatively new departure for occult thought. Margot Adler, herself a feminist witch, admits that there is a strong patriarchal tradition within occultism.[6] One reason for the New Age interest in feminism may be that many women dissatisfied with the aggressive atheism of much of the feminist movement turned to Neo-Paganism and the New Age in search of a spiritual dimension. In so doing they would have brought their feminist concerns with them. Another reason is the perceived relationship between patriarchal oppression of women and technological exploitation of nature. If the two are as closely linked as some commentators insist,[7] the strong New Age concern for the latter might be expected to spill over into the former.

Some New Agers also campaign for minority rights, including gay rights and the rights of native peoples. Again the New Age support for gay rights may be, in part, a result of its greater openness to gay men and women. A number of gays who have been rebuffed by the churches (and other religious bodies) have found a spiritual home in the New Age. As for the rights of native peoples, this issue is tied up with New Age concern for the environment, the New Age ideal of a decentralized society living in harmony with nature, and the growing interest in shamanism (and other magico-religious practices from primal religions) as a New Age psychotechnology.

(d) How influential is New Age politics?

I have already commented on the possible de-politicizing effect of involvement in the New Age. Consider the case of the actress Shirley MacLaine. Prior to her emergence as a leading spokesperson for the New Age she was an active political campaigner, opposing America's involvement in Vietnam and campaigning for civil rights, women's rights, and environmental protection. In 1968 and 1972 she was a delegate to the Democratic Party conventions. These political concerns are now overshadowed by her involvement in the New Age. She now focusses on personal rather than social transformation.

Significantly Mark Satin, one of the major political theorists of the New Age, has now virtually disowned his New Age background. Since 1983 he has been the editor of *New Options*, a journal which specializes in post-liberal social critiques. He now views the more radical aspects of the New Age political agenda as utopian and unrealistic.

On the other hand, the New Age movement has made a real impact on western attitudes. In particular environmentalism is an issue on which New Agers are taken seriously. Their widespread involvement in environmental pressure groups gives them a degree of genuine political influence.

Nevertheless the political influence of the New Age remains far less than many Christian commentators fear. Their reputation for wielding considerable clandestine political influence has grown partly out of an uncritical acceptance of the most extravagant New Age claims and partly out of a fear of political conspiracies. It seems that the numbers of New Agers are still well below what is needed to achieve a critical mass. Even if the critical mass view of politics is correct, I suspect the figures published by New Agers are unduly optimistic. Given the power of tradition, far more than 20 per cent of the population would have to be involved to bring about radical change from the grassroots in a democratic fashion.

2. ENVIRONMENTALISM AND GREEN SPIRITUALITY

The global environment crisis is arguably the most serious issue facing humankind at the end of the twentieth century. Environmental concern has succeeded in bringing together men and women of every creed, colour, and political persuasion to struggle against a common threat.

It has also become clear that the New Age movement has a particular stake in environmentalism. For some years individuals and groups have been promoting various kinds of Green spirituality. So strong is the New Age stake here that one Christian critic has been moved to write that environmentalism 'is one of the most powerful influences leading people into the New Age movement'.[8]

That comment fails to recognize the remarkable diversity of environmentalism. The issue has become common ground for men and women of every political and religious persuasion. David Pepper, who has made several studies of environmentalism, now classifies it into seven streams distinguished by differing political outlooks.[9]

In fact, the environmental movement is deeply divided over Green spirituality or deep ecology. Many eco-socialists are suspicious of this approach (especially in Germany, where they recall with horror the Nazi use of earth mysticism). The bitterness of this division is made clear by one leading eco-socialist, Murray Bookchin:

> The greatest difference that is now emerging in the so-called 'Ecology Movement' today is between a vague, formless, self-contradictory, invertebrate thing called 'Deep Ecology', and a long-developing, coherent, socially-oriented body of ideas that is best called Social Ecology. Deep Ecology has parachuted into our midst quite recently from the sun-belt's bizarre mix of Hollywood and Disneyland, re-born Christianity, spiced homilies from Taoism, Buddhism, spirituality and so on and so forth.

He dismisses it as 'ecolala' which he defines as 'nebulous nature-worship with its suspicious bouquet of wood-sprites and fertility rites, its animist, shamanistic figures and post-industrial paganism'.[10]

Equally tendentious, but more descriptive are the following comments from Australian philosopher John Passmore:

> 'Depth', . . . , implies an acceptance of primitivism and mysticism, a willingness to revert to a state of affairs where the world, except for a few colonies of hunters, was a vast wilderness, the rejection, as 'speciesism', of any preference for human interests over the interests of any other species.[11]

Deep ecology is a remarkably eclectic force within the environmental movement. Its advocates have ransacked the history of western culture for anything which might add weight to their view that the spiritual dimension is an integral part of the environmental problem and that learning to respect the environment will entail something akin to worship. At times this takes on an almost ludicrous note as when Puritan use of analogies drawn from nature is cited as evidence of a suppressed desire to worship nature.[12]

3. TRANSFORMING THE MARKET PLACE

Politics may be important but it is only one dimension of our social life. Equally important, at least for western society, is the economic dimension, the world of business, the market place. To what extent has the New Age penetrated this aspect of our corporate life?

As in the case of New Age politics, the stress on personal transformation militates against a concerted effort to re-work the market place. It favours instead a process of gradual diffusion as individual New Agers begin to carry the effects of their personal transformation into the workplace. Thus the socio-economic structure of the New Age will govern which aspects of the business world are most affected by its insights.

Certain industries have seen a much greater New Age influence than others. The fact that a disproportionately high percentage of Neo-Pagans and New Agers have found employment in areas such as systems analysis, computer software and information technology would lead one to expect that any influence they might have upon working conditions would be greatest in these areas. Anecdotal evidence suggests that this is the case but firm statistical evidence is still lacking. Is it coincidental that Boulder, Colorado, is a centre of both the computer industry and New Age activity? It has even been suggested that the pyramidal architecture of parts of Silicon Valley in California owes as much to ancient beliefs about the occult powers of pyramids as to modern art!

(a) New Age businesses

While the New Age has apparently made some headway within the computer industry it is still far from transforming the market place from within. An alternative approach which appeals to some New Age entrepreneurs is that of setting up businesses along lines consistent with New Age philosophies. Many of these are little more than cottage industries in which a handful of workers, often organized on a co-operative basis rather than in a hierarchy, manage to keep alive some of the traditional crafts.

More are in the retail trade. But again most of these are relatively small operations existing primarily to serve the New Age market. One firm which does not fit this generalization but which is held up by New Agers as an example of their business principles in action is the Body Shop.[13]

The Body Shop specializes in selling natural cosmetics based on traditional formulae which have not been tested on animals. Packaging is kept to a minimum: the paper used is recycled and the bottles are re-fillable. Thus both its products and the way in which they are sold reflect the New Age's concern for the environment.

However the Body Shop has also adopted a non-hierarchical decentralized structure. It operates on a franchise system rather than maintaining all the branches under a single central structure. Employees who began as salespersons have been encouraged and given the necessary support to begin their own franchise. Furthermore the company's concern for people extends beyond its own employees to its suppliers in the Third World, e.g., supporting the work of a number of Boys Towns in India and a paper making project in Nepal.

Its founder Anita Roddick does not despise profit: it creates jobs and can be an agent for social change. But she rejects the contemporary tendency to see profit as an end in itself. Instead she has inverted the relative status accorded to people and profit by secular society: for her people are more important than profits.

(b) Management consultancy

The main way in which the New Age has made an impact on the business world is through its presence in the management consultancy field. In recent decades there has been a meteoric growth in the number of organizations offering courses and seminars designed to improve your performance in every aspect of management and salesmanship.

A significant factor in the increasing popularity of such courses has been the contemporary obsession with self-improvement. The Human Potential Movement has had a very powerful influence on American society at just this point. And because of the dominance of the United States in the world economy, American attitudes have been exported to every country of the western world (and are now rapidly penetrating the former Eastern bloc).

Of course many of the workshops on offer are relatively harmless. For example, time management is something that many more people could benefit from.

The point at which questions might begin to be asked about New Age management is where eastern mysticism and occult practices are packaged as techniques for improving your management skills. Since New Agers tend to be pragmatic about such techniques they are unlikely to see a problem in this. After all, if creative visualization can improve your sales levels it must be a useful technique for salesmen to learn. However, others might well question the morality of covertly imposing religious practices on members of others faiths or none.

But does this happen? The short answer is 'yes'. Examples include the presentation of TM as a scientific method of relaxation when, in fact, it is a form of Bhakti Yoga with similarities to the practices of the Hare Krishna movement. In this form it has been taught to managers in a number of multi-national corporations. Similarly some management consultants are encouraging the use of the *I Ching* as a tool for creative problem-solving.

In the UK, New Ager and former business executive Michael Wolff now runs a successful management consultancy business, the Results Partnership. His clients have included a number of well-known British firms including TV-am, Allied Dunbar, Dixons and Woolworth. Another New Age consultancy firm, Pathfinder, offers a specialist astrological careers advice service. The Findhorn Foundation now offers a course in Intuitive Leadership.

Many of the techniques highlighted in previous chapters are being imported into the world of business. Senior executives are increasingly encouraging their middle-management to attend such courses in their continual search for anything which might give their firm that edge over its competitors which might make the difference between survival and bankruptcy. In the United States there has been a rash of court cases arising from

Christians objecting to being disciplined for refusing to take part in courses they regarded as dubious. A recent case in Scotland suggests that this may be spreading to the UK.[14]

Does this tendency presage a New Age transformation in the world of work? Ironically such courses may actually be co-opted by the structures of the business world to reinforce the status quo. One of the attractions of EST to business executives was its capacity to produce an aggressively self-centred executive with no inconvenient moral qualms about product, sales technique, or the conditions of workers.

4. TRANSFORMING CULTURE

(a) New Age music

This is a very loose term which does not, in fact, refer to a particular style of music. Originally it was applied to any music which its composers, performers or promoters felt was helpful as an aid to meditation. It now includes a great deal of material which has been produced merely to cash in on this lucrative market. In addition to material composed specifically for use in a New Age context, New Age music labels have adopted such things as plainsong, some folk music, some minimalist music, and natural noises (e.g., the sea, whale songs). I have even heard of instrumental arrangements of Graham Kendrick songs being presented as New Age music!

Typically New Age music is characterless and unmemorable. In order to be successful background music for meditation it must be relatively simple, quiet, and uniform. This rules out both strong melody lines and discords. Rhythm is permissible but must be simple (some New Age teachers use drum beats to synchronize heartbeats and/or brainwaves in the belief that this can enhance meditation). Typical musical instruments include harps and flutes (or similar high-pitched wind instruments such as pan pipes). The current wave of fascination with primitive religion has recently brought the didgeridoo to prominence (as an alternative source of rhythm).

What makes a piece of music New Age is the use to which it is put.

(b) New Age in the media

The New Age phenomenon may be encountered through the media in a number of ways. The most obvious is direct documentary coverage of New Age, Neo-Pagan, and occult activities. During the past year (1990–1991) British television networks have broadcast programmes covering many aspects of the New Age. Apart from an entire series devoted to it on Channel 4, it has featured in documentaries on mythology, alternative medicine, deep ecology, Glastonbury, and psychosynthesis. The attitude adopted by such documentaries ranges from extreme scepticism to warm appreciation, with the majority apparently trying to steer a middle course of objectivity and neutrality. Of course the very fact that television now presents such material without critical comment suggests that it be taken seriously (at least no less seriously than any of the other religious or philosophical opinions which are broadcast).

New Age activities also achieve media coverage by virtue of the media's fascination with the idiosyncracies of the rich, the famous, and the powerful. The revelation that Nancy Reagan consulted an astrologer while her husband was President of the United States is typical. More recently a report in the Sunday Express Magazine cites more than two dozen celebrities as participants in New Age activities. Of course, as with most such popular reports, its contents range from the well-established (Shirley MacLaine's use of crystals) to the frankly ludicrous (attempting to connect Margaret Thatcher with the New Age on the strength of her use of homoeopathic remedies and her enjoyment of 'a thoroughly good, strong massage to get the circulation going').

A third way in which we meet New Age ideas through the media might be called close encounters of a fictional kind. Many science fiction and fantasy films contain implicit or explicit reference to New Age ideas. For example, the Force depicted in *Star Wars* is recognizable as one of the New Age concepts of the divine (and the clear connection between the martial arts of the Jedi Knights and spirituality has parallels in many eastern martial arts). A more recent (and explicit) example is the film *Communion* based on the book by Whitley Streiber: it details contact with the pilots of UFOs (a recurring theme amongst some New Age groups).

(c) Science fiction and fantasy: literature for a New Age

The New Age dimension in SF and fantasy films is, of course, derived from the burgeoning literature of those genres. Many authors in these fields are grappling with concepts which, in earlier generations, would have been clearly recognized as religious. As a result Margot Adler suggests that, 'science fiction and fantasy probably come closer than any other literature to systematically exploring the central concerns of Neo-Pagans and Witches'.[15] Thus it is hardly surprising to find in a 1985 survey of American Neo-Pagans that nearly ten per cent were drawn to occultism by reading SF.[16] Nor is it surprising to find that a number of these authors have personal connections with some form of occultism or mysticism. The most notorious example is L. Ron Hubbard (whose spirituality was influenced by Aleister Crowley) who, in addition to being a successful SF writer, was the founder of the Church of Scientology. Robert Anton Wilson (author of the *Illuminati* trilogy) is a leading figure of the Discordian movement in American occultism. In the UK, Terry Pratchett has appeared as a guest speaker for the Pagan Federation. One of the most distinguished writers in these fields, Ursula Le Guin, describes herself as 'an inconsistent Taoist, and a consistent unChristian'.

5. TRANSFORMING THE CLASSROOM

Many Christian parents have been disturbed by Frank Peretti's fictional portrayal of current trends in education. His novels *This Present Darkness* and *Piercing the Darkness* depict, in a highly sensational form, what he regards as New Age inroads into the American educational system. New educational methods are presented as part of an occult conspiracy to win the minds and hearts of our children. Nor has he confined these accusations to his fiction. In an interview last year he asserted that, 'In the States there's a tremendous influx of New Age occultism into the public education system. There are curricula materials teaching little kids how to be psychic'.[17]

The New Age movement certainly has an interest in education. Marilyn Ferguson criticizes the American education system as one of the least dynamic institutions in her society. Following the lead of such radical educators as Ivan Illich and Paolo Freire, she accuses traditional education systems of generating considerable anxiety and even illness amongst students.

(a) Transpersonal education

Our rapidly changing world culture demands a new and more flexible approach to education. Ferguson presents a thumbnail sketch of a transpersonal education in which 'the learner is encouraged to be awake and autonomous, to question, to explore all the corners and crevices of conscious experience, to seek meaning, to test outer limits, to check out frontiers and depths of self.'[18]

The New Age ideal for education seems entirely laudable. The components of Ferguson's transpersonal education, include systems theory, greater reliance on intuition, greater stress on innovation and creativity, more use of multi-cultural materials, and a commitment to improving the pupils' self-image. However, Zen meditation and other psychotechnologies also appear on her New Age curriculum.

Others have put theory into practice, setting up their own alternative schools. One American example is the University of the Trees. This is a New Age community founded in Santa Cruz, California, in 1973. It runs a training programme and publishes a range of books and other materials relating to transpersonal education. In this way it has pioneered the use of meditation as a teaching technique both in private New Age schools and, to some extent, within the American state education system.

(b) The New Age in British schools

The New Age movement has, so far, made relatively little impact on the state education system in the UK. However, techniques similar to those pilloried by Peretti are increasingly being used in this country.

In particular guided imagery and guided fantasy are beginning to appear in a number of subjects. These are visualization techniques in which the goal is imaginative participation in some story or script. The participant may be encouraged to seek wisdom by engaging in a conversation with one of the characters in the script.

Leading the field are some of the more experiential approaches to Personal and Social Education (PSE), and Religious Education. This is probably because of the impetus of the 1988 Education Reform Act which requires that schools shall promote 'the spiritual . . . development of pupils'.[19] However, similar techniques have also found their way into subjects as diverse as physical education, art and music, English literature, and even biology.

Such practices are often promoted as ways of stimulating imagination and creativity. Thus they are aids to the fuller development of the human potential of schoolchildren. Some advocates go even further and suggest that this is a valid alternative way of knowing the world.[20]

Visualization is also promoted because of its supposed therapeutic and remedial value. Such techniques are increasingly used by coaches to suppress tension and anxiety prior to a sporting event. They are also used to help create a more positive frame of mind or overcome some personal difficulty such as shyness or a stammer.

But the most common justification is pragmatic: the techniques produce positive results. Specifically, they lead to improved discipline, greater cooperation and participation, and a general improvement in academic performance.[21] Such exercises also hold out the promise of an enjoyable and relatively easy alternative to more traditional lesson forms.[22]

In spite of these arguments, I believe there is real cause for concern on several counts.

These are very powerful psychological tools. Most of the writing in this area is far too sanguine about the risks involved in undertaking the inner journey.[23] Contrary to the assumptions of some educationists, it is relatively easy to evoke extremely profound and disturbing psychological experiences through guided fantasy. Very few teachers are trained to handle such situations. Furthermore the counselling which may be necessary can be time consuming. The pressures of most school timetables would prevent them giving the time necessary.

There is also the danger of indoctrination. The most successful fantasy scripts emerge from the author's imagination and stimulate the imaginations of the participants, bypassing their critical faculties. Even if teachers resist the temptation to promote their beliefs in this way, there is no protection from their unconscious beliefs and presuppositions. This danger is heightened when the material used in the guided fantasy is drawn from religious sources. The stories and myths of the world's religions are a rich source of scripts for guided fantasy. But what is happening when people approach these stories through guided fantasy? Advocates of guided fantasy assume that it offers a safe way of gaining some insight into religious faith and practice. However, as Ignatius of Loyola discovered, such use of the imagination may actually be a very powerful way of participating in a religious tradition.

Nor is the danger of indoctrination confined to the exercise itself. Such exercises can evoke profound experiences which demand interpretation. There is a real possibility of unintentional indoctrination whenever the teacher has to talk through such an experience with a pupil. In fact, so real is the risk of indoctrination that one leading advocate of guided fantasy questions whether it should be permitted in the context of religious education.[24]

These psychological dangers call into question the wisdom of using guided fantasy without careful training and supervision. However, from a Christian perspective, the potential spiritual dangers are even more disturbing.

Many Christians regard demonic influence or possession as the primary spiritual danger of such practices. This is the scenario envisaged by Peretti in *Piercing the Darkness*: a young girl becomes possessed as a result of guided fantasy exercises designed to put her in touch with her inner wisdom.

We should not dismiss this fear out of hand. On the contrary, even Jung recognized the possibility of irrational psychic forces erupting out of the unconscious to take possession of the conscious mind.[25] Christianity has traditionally affirmed the objective reality of such forces without making the naive assumption that these forces are natural and ultimately benign.

However, more serious than the possibility of demonic possession is the way in which such techniques reinforce our culture's obsession with self-image and self-affirmation. Guided fantasy may be a legitimate tool of spiritual development when used with appropriate safeguards. More commonly it is used to promote self-reliance and self-fulfillment. From a Christian perspective, it may actually promote a godlessness which may be described thus:

> True godlessness is not the abstract denial of the existence of God, but the denial of one's own dependence upon God, that is, the denial of one's own existential being as God's creature. Thus unbelief is man's fundamental sin. And unbelief means to persevere in the principle of self-justification.[26]

Far from offering a harmless and enjoyable way of gaining insight into religion such techniques may actually be the antithesis of Christian faith.

5

Transforming Science?

1. SPIRITUALITY FOR A TECHNOLOGICAL AGE

The New Age movement clearly draws many of its insights from pre-Christian paganism. This has led, not unnaturally, to the accusation that New Agers want to put the clock back to before the beginning of the scientific revolution.

New Age thinkers have certainly made negative judgements about important aspects of contemporary society. They celebrate the impending disintegration of industrial society and a radical transformation of science.

However, for the most part, they would deny the charge that they are opposed to science or technology. Even those individuals who are drawn to the primitivism of some forms of Neo-Paganism tend not to be opposed to science as such. Indeed Margot Adler suggests that 'the majority of Neo-Pagans are optimistic about the uses of science and modern technology'.[1]

Generally speaking New Agers are optimistic about the prospects of transforming science and technology. They do not want to give up the fruits of technological progress. On the contrary they claim that their objections are to the wrong use of technology to oppress others and to harm the earth.

Like Christians who are engaged in science, scientifically minded New Agers and Pagans draw a distinction between science and scientism (or scientolatry), the latter being one of the forms of dogmatic secular humanism. For example, one Pagan interviewed by Adler insists that 'Science is a method, a technique. And technology is very useful. The problem is not with the tools, but with this idolatrous attitude toward science, this secular religion that denies all other aspects of being human'.[2]

New Agers and Pagans want to rehumanize science and technology. They want to enrich our society by reminding us that there is a spiritual dimension to our existence.

Many of them also regard New Age spirituality as a genuinely scientific approach to this spiritual dimension. They see the New Age as drawing its inspiration at key points from the findings of modern science. The psychological explorations of Jung and others are one important foundation for New Age thought. But New Agers also claim to draw on evolutionary theory, ecology, systems theory, relativity, and quantum mechanics. They see themselves as in the process of developing a spirituality uniquely suited to a scientific age.

2. EVOLUTION: BIOLOGICAL AND COSMIC

(a) Darwin and the Great Chain of Being

Contrary to popular belief, Darwin did not originate the idea of evolution. Several significant volumes on the subject were published prior to the appearance of *The Origin of Species*. In fact, it is arguable that the germ of the idea can be traced back to classical philosophy. 'Why, it's all in Lucretius!' wrote Matthew Arnold in bewilderment at the debate over Darwin.

That germ took the form of the Great Chain of Being. It was commonly believed that all of reality from the lowliest particle of dust to the loftiest spirit was inter-related in a hierarchical structure emanating from God. The idea is embedded in the way we speak: we still talk of 'higher' mammals and 'lower' invertebrates. It seems natural to think of disembodied spirits as 'higher' than embodied spirits (human beings) and those in turn as 'higher' than non-rational animals.

For centuries it remained an important metaphysical principle. Western Christian theology successfully Christianized it by making a decisive break in the chain between God and creation. The development which led ultimately to Darwinism was a much greater emphasis on historical providence following the Reformation: this doctrine was gradually secularized into the Enlightenment doctrine of progress. By the turn of the nineteenth century it was widely assumed that human progress and divine providence were one and the same thing. Evolutionary speculation was merely the extension of progress downwards to the nonhuman.

Biological evolution transformed the Great Chain of Being from a metaphysical principle into an historical principle. Darwin's particular contribution was the suggestion of a mechanism by which evolution could proceed. With *The Origin of Species* evolution became a scientific hypothesis.

(b) The spiritualization of evolution

Almost immediately other thinkers began to seek ways of setting evolution free from its scientific shackles. It was soon taken up as a potential model for spiritual development.

One such attempt was that of Helena Blavatsky, founder of the Theosophical Society and an important forerunner of many of today's New Agers. She tried to reconcile the Hindu concepts of reincarnation and karma with the idea of evolution. Souls progress through successive reincarnations until they have gained sufficient insight to escape from the cycle of life and death.

An altogether more sophisticated application of evolutionary ideas to the development of the human spirit was made by the French philosopher Henri Bergson. His philosophy was to become one of the building blocks of Teilhard de Chardin's vision of a cosmos evolving towards God.

A third effort worth mentioning is that of the obscure English philosopher, Olaf Stapledon. In spite of his obscurity, he ranks with H. G. Wells as one of the greatest science fiction novelists of all times. His novels, while largely unread by the general public, have been ransacked by subsequent generations of writers in search of inspiration. Robert Heinlein and Ron Hubbard, together with many of today's leading science fiction writers, owe a great deal to him. His greatest work, *Star Maker* (published in 1937), is a massive poetic account of a cosmic vision of evolution from the level of humanity upwards. In it, the evolution of consciousness transcends the individual: planets, galaxies, and ultimately the universe as a whole becomes conscious. Just such a vision is integral to the New Age world-view.

(c) Teilhard's vision of cosmic evolution

Important as the above have been in shaping New Age thought none can compare with the Jesuit priest Pierre Teilhard de Chardin. Forbidden to publish his evolutionary speculations during his lifetime, his work has posthumously become the single greatest influence upon many leading New Agers.[3]

Teilhard was one of the most distinguished scientists of his Order. With something like 150 scientific papers to his name, he was widely regarded as a seminal figure in the study of human palaeontology.

The recurring theme of his forbidden writings was his quest for a synthesis between Roman Catholic theology and evolutionary thought. Like St Thomas Aquinas he believed passionately in the unity of all knowledge: thus he insisted that theology and modern science can and should be coherent. This was essentially an exercise in natural theology, taking as its starting-point the concept of evolution.

Initially the universe is chaotic: a flux of elementary particles in a state of maximum multiplicity and simplicity. However, God has implanted in these elements an urge towards unity and, thus, towards greater complexity and consciousness. This point was described by Teilhard as the starting-point and key of his entire system. It is also the very point which caused greatest offence to the biological establishment. It amounts to a flat contradiction of the neo-Darwinian consensus that evolution is undirected.

The immediate implication of the relationship Teilhard establishes between complexity and consciousness is that all entities are dipolar. They possess both a 'without', a degree of physical organization or complexity, and a 'within', a degree of consciousness. Both dimensions evolve as simple entities combined together in increasingly complex structures.

The notion that a sub-atomic particle might have a rudimentary consciousness (a belief known as panpsychism) seems strange to many people. However, it is a consequence of Teilhard's belief in a Chain of Being: nature does not proceed by leaps; everything occurs continuously and gradually. Consciousness clearly exists in humankind. If it is related to physical complexity in the way Teilhard believed, then it must have emerged gradually from some proto-consciousness.

Gradually, over periods of billions of years, molecules became increasingly complex until, at the level of proteins, a critical stage was reached: the complex molecules began to exhibit the capacity to replicate. Life had emerged. A new phase in the evolution of the cosmos had begun: biogenesis. Gradually life covered the earth and gave rise to the biosphere. The emergence of life represented a quantum leap in the degree of complexity which could be achieved. The leading edge of evolution moved from the physical to the biological sphere.

Within the evolutionary history of life, Teilhard saw clear evidence of progress: 'a persistent and clearly defined thrust of animal forms towards species with more sensitive and elaborate nervous systems'.[4] This phase of 'cephalization' reached its climax with the emergence of animals with a central nervous system. Another new level of complexity has been reached from which yet another quantum leap in evolution becomes possible. Through the process of 'cerebration', the gradual evolutionary increase in complexity and convolution of mammalian brains, the scene is set for anthropogenesis – the emergence of humankind.

The evolutionary process continues amongst these proto-humans. It takes on a social dimension. Yet another level of complexity comes into view. Notice the recurring pattern at each evolutionary level: the climax of one level becomes the fundamental building block of the next. Thus atoms are the building blocks for molecules, which are the building blocks for the simplest living organisms, which in turn are the building blocks for ever more complex organisms.

Now with the first humans evolution takes a new tack. Full human consciousness permits the possibility of personal relationships and the emergence of social structures. This led Teilhard to speculate about the present and future of the evolutionary process. He envisaged the emergence of a conscious planetary organism (the *noosphere*) of which individual human beings are the constituent parts:

> the *planetization* of Mankind, associated with a *closed* grouping of people: Mankind, born on this planet and spread over its entire surface, coming gradually to form around its earthly matrix a single, major organic unity, *enclosed upon itself*; a single hyper-complex, hyper-centred, hyper-conscious archmolecule, co-extensive with the heavenly body on which it was born.[5]

Looking even beyond the emergence of the noosphere, he notes that the logic of his evolutionary vision with its law of recurrence demands an end-point:

> the existence, at the upper term of cosmic convergence, of a transcendent centre of unification, 'Omega Point'. Unless this focus-point, which gathers things together and ensures their irreversibility, does in fact exist, the law of evolutionary recurrence cannot hold good to the very end.[6]

This is precisely what makes his evolutionary vision so attractive to New Agers – it is fundamentally optimistic, it envisages a rosy future for humankind, and they can read into the information explosion of the past decade clear signs of its coming to pass.

3. GAIA: THE LIVING EARTH

Teilhard's work was visionary. Unlike Darwin he showed little interest in observational evidence to back up his speculation. It is sometimes suggested that this omission is made good by Jim Lovelock's *Gaia Hypothesis*; that there is empirical evidence for an emerging planetary consciousness.

(a) The hypothesis

In his first book on the Gaia hypothesis James Lovelock offered the following working definition: 'a complex entity involving the Earth's biosphere, atmosphere, oceans, and soil; the totality constituting a feedback or cybernetic system which seeks an optimal physical and chemical environment for life on this planet'.[7]

In prosaic terms the Gaia hypothesis asserts that, as life evolved on the earth, a complex network of interactions emerged between living creatures and their non-living environment. Furthermore these interactions, when taken together, have the effect of stabilizing aspects of the environment essential for life (e.g., climate, atmospheric chemistry, and salinity of the oceans). This represents a radical change from conventional wisdom since it proposes the existence of biological control mechanisms governing aspects of the environment which were formerly regarded as quite independent of life.

In a series of books and articles Lovelock has presented a wide range of evidence in favour of his hypothesis. He has suggested plausible biological mechanisms to explain the stability of the earth's surface temperature (in spite of a gradual increase in solar radiation), the low salinity of the oceans, and the chemical composition of the atmosphere. Most important, he has made testable predictions about the behaviour of this hypothetical biological control system.

At present the observational evidence for or against Gaia is not conclusive. Some scientists find the approach helpful: it has certainly made some earth scientists more aware that they may need to consider biological factors. However, for many scientists, Gaia is highly controversial.

The roots of this controversy lie in Lovelock's more provocative remarks about his hypothesis. On occasion he has likened this global environmental control system to an organism, specifically 'the largest living organism'.[8] But his most sweeping statement of the hypothesis must surely be, 'the Gaia hypothesis supposes the Earth to be alive'.[9]

Such language only serves to alienate his fellow scientists. They see in it either a woefully inadequate understanding of what is meant by life or an implicit claim that the environment is consciously controlled by some entity which has emerged from the sum of living creatures. Even Lovelock's close associate, Lynn Margulis, has taken issue with him on this point.[10]

(b) The myth

Gaia is controversial amongst scientists because Lovelock insists that it means the earth as a whole is a single living organism. But it is precisely this aspect of the Gaia hypothesis which has proved so attractive to sections of the New Age community. They see it as potential scientific confirmation of the New Age belief that something akin to planetary consciousness is emerging. Thus Sir George Trevelyan has proclaimed it an appropriate myth for our post-industrial age.[11]

The most elaborate New Age interpretation of Gaia is Peter Russell's book *The Awakening Earth*. Russell is a management consultant and author who has been active in popularizing Transcendental Meditation. In fact, only a relatively small part of his book is devoted to the kinds of issues tackled by Lovelock. He integrates the Gaia hypothesis into a larger evolutionary cosmology informed mainly by Teilhard de Chardin (and his Hindu counterpart Sri Aurobindo). This becomes the launch pad for what is, in effect, an introduction to New Age thought.

Russell believes that Gaia is only just on the threshold of consciousness. This is directly related to the New Age expectation of a global transformation. We stand at a critical moment in the history of evolution. He suggests that there is an analogy between the human population explosion of recent decades and the rapid multiplication of neurones in the brain of a human embryo. There will soon be as many human beings as there are neurones in the average human brain. In human development, the rapid multiplication of neurones gives way to the rapid multiplication of synaptic connections between them and the awakening of consciousness. So it is with the Earth – it is possible that the explosion of information technology will result in a planetary brain with humans as the individual neurones. But that evolution depends critically upon the choices we make in the next few decades: 'We appear to be at a historical cusp, wavering between two mutually exclusive directions: breaking through to become a global social super-organism; or breaking down into chaos and possible extinction'.[12]

Like most New Agers, Russell is optimistic that the human

race will rise to the challenge: 'As worldwide communication capabilities become increasingly complex, society is beginning to look more and more like a planetary nervous system. The global brain is being activated'.[13]

The Gaia hypothesis inadvertently supports New Age speculation about planetary consciousness. It also asserts the interconnectedness of all terrestrial organisms together with their physical environment. Some New Agers extrapolate from that level to the cosmos as a whole and imagine that Lovelock has provided scientific legitimation of the view that *all* spiritual and material realities are mutually interdependent.

However, there are further reasons for its attraction to New Agers. The very name is replete with connotations for anyone with a classical education or an interest in paganism or feminist spirituality. Gaia was the Universal Mother of classical Greek religion. As Theodore Roszak, a perceptive commentator on the New Age movement, notes, 'the image of Earth as a living personality has sounded strong existential chords'.[14]

This might lead one to expect the widespread celebration of the Gaia hypothesis by New Agers and Neo-Pagans. In fact, interest in the hypothesis is surprisingly patchy.[15] There are a number of New Agers who use a metaphysical or mystical reading of the Gaia hypothesis as the basis for beliefs about planetary consciousness.[16] However, many others, who might have been expected to exploit Lovelock's work, ignore it completely.

Why is this? My own surmise is that, while some New Agers find the connection with modern science helpful, many do not see any need to link their philosophical speculations with a scientific hypothesis.

There are, effectively, two Gaias. The hypothesis proposed by Lovelock may or may not have potential as a piece of science. Alongside it, and often confused with it, is the myth of Gaia, the earth goddess. The latter is attractive to that relatively small sub-section of Neo-Pagans who find fulfillment in the worship of the deities of classical Greece. Many other Neo-Pagans and New Agers have their own parallel myths which they find more satisfying: for them Gaia and Lovelock are likely to remain only a footnote.

4. BIOLOGY BEYOND MECHANISM

The success of modern biology has largely been built upon
the assumption that living creatures may be regarded as very
complex machines. However such an assumption is anathema
to New Agers. They regard it as leading to a reductionist view
of life. By contrast they insist that living systems must be
regarded as greater than the sum of their parts. From a Christian perspective there is certainly some attraction in this view.
Christians and New Agers are agreed upon the necessity of
avoiding ways of thinking which reduce the most important
aspects of life to mere by-products of machinery.

But does this mean a return to a vitalist theory of life? These
theories asserted that, in order to make the mechanisms go,
some additional element had to be present: a life force, or soul.
This force, or entity, inhabited and animated the body. Many
Christians still think in these terms (at least of human life).
Some New Agers (particularly those inspired by theosophy)
also tend to see human beings as spirits temporarily embarked
upon a physical pilgrimage. But, however attractive these
suggestions might seem, their dualistic view of mind and matter
has proved notoriously difficult to relate in any coherent way
to the biological sciences.

This is why a new holistic approach to biology, developed
by Rupert Sheldrake, has been hailed by many New Agers as
a potential solution. He proposes that *morphogenetic* fields
(analogous to the electromagnetic and gravitational fields of
physics) govern the development of biological forms. Behind
this is a suspicion that the structure of DNA alone cannot
account for the variety of form observed in any living creature.

He suggests that these fields are inherently evolutionary: a
kind of collective memory of form. Thus,

> The formative activity of the fields is not determined by
> timeless mathematical laws . . . but by the actual forms taken
> up by previous members of the species. The more often a
> pattern of development is repeated, the more probable it is
> that it will be followed again. The fields are the means by

which the habits of the species are built up, maintained and inherited.[17]

Sheldrake insists that his hypothesis is testable. For example, when a new substance is crystallized for the first time there will be no previous examples for it to draw on for a preferred form. After its first appearance, subsequent crystallizations should tend to resemble the first and the substance should become gradually easier to crystallize. In fact, just such a phenomenon has often been commented upon by organic chemists. However, they have an alternative explanation: fragments of previous crystals are gradually transferred from laboratory to laboratory by visiting chemists (by acting as crystallization nuclei, these fragments would make subsequent crystallizations easier).

Because it is testable, Sheldrake's hypothesis does warrant examination by the scientific community. However, it has implications which make it attractive to New Agers. In addition to its holistic perspective, it could function as a mechanism for the hundredth monkey effect described in the previous chapter. It can readily be generalized from a testable scientific theory into a metaphysical explanation for everything. In his most recent book, Sheldrake has succumbed to that temptation. In addition to biological form, he uses it to explain memory, habits, social organization, Gaia, and even religion.

5. THE TAO AND PHYSICS

Another aspect of modern science which has captured the imagination of New Agers is the revolution in physics which began at the turn of the century. Since classical physics was fundamental to the mechanistic view of reality which they dislike, these developments are widely hailed as marking science's own realization of the limitations of its foundations. Thus Marilyn Ferguson can assert that 'the discoveries of science have begun to make sense of mystical experiences people have been describing for millenia. They suggest that we can tap into that order of reality *behind* the world of appearances'.[18]

One of the most ardent advocates of this opinion is the nuclear physicist, Fritjof Capra. He has outlined the mystical potential of modern physics in his popular book *The Tao of Physics*. His basic thesis is that 'The basic oneness of the universe is not only the central characteristic of the mystical experience, but is also one of the most important revelations of modern physics'.[19] He attempts to demonstrate this point by examining certain aspects of relativity theory and quantum mechanics.

(a) Space-time and relativism

Einstein's Principle of Relativity states that the laws of physics take the same form in any inertial frame of reference. In making this assertion he was denying the absoluteness of space and time.

It is a simple assertion but it has far-reaching consequences for our understanding of the world around us. For example, from being qualitatively different absolutes space and time become inextricably linked in space-time. This means that we have to redefine very carefully what is meant by the simultaneity of two events. Denying the absoluteness of time also means that we can no longer define a unique present: past, present, and future as commonly understood become problematic.

Relativity theory does two things. Negatively, it forces us to move from a universal to a local perspective: we can no longer expect to measure the absolute location of an event in space and time. All we can do is locate it relative to some local inertial frame. Positively, it enables us to relate the measurements made in different inertial frames.

The fact that all measurements must be relative to some inertial frame implies that there can be many different answers to a question such as 'what is the location and velocity of X?' Capra apparently ignores the fact that all these answers can be related and infers from their multiplicity that 'space and time become merely elements of the language a particular observer uses for his description of the phenomena'.[20] At the beginning of his chapter on space-time he extends this inference even further:

Modern physics has confirmed most dramatically one of the basic ideas of Eastern mysticism; that all the concepts we use to describe nature are limited, that they are not features of reality, as we tend to believe, but creations of the mind; parts of the map, not of the territory.[21]

In other words, reality is indeterminate and unstructured until it is ordered by the human mind.

But this is a highly idiosyncratic interpretation of relativity theory. By contrast, the dominant interpretation is deterministic. Time is interpreted as merely a misunderstood spatial dimension, and reality is presented as a static ensemble of world-lines in space-time. There is no past, present and future worth speaking of. Strangely Capra attempts to co-opt this interpretation in spite of the fact that it contradicts his earlier inferences. He suggests that this suppression of time is somehow analogous to the mystical goal of liberation from time.[22]

One corollary of the Principle of Relativity which has caught the popular imagination is the equivalence of mass and energy ($E=mc^2$). Capra tells us more than once that this means 'mass is nothing but a form of energy'.[23] But this is a tendentious oversimplification. Why not say energy is nothing but a form of mass? The answer is, because Capra is a Taoist: in Taoist metaphysics the cosmos is permeated by *chi* (a life-giving aether or energy). He is reading into relativity theory an interpretation which suits his metaphysics.

(b) Quantum mechanics and monism

Einstein was a philosophical realist. By contrast many of the founding fathers of quantum mechanics were idealists and, as you might expect, Capra finds this a more congenial source for his mystical speculation.

Strange things happen at the quantum level! One of its best known peculiarities is wave-particle duality. This does not mean (as is sometimes suggested) that such entities are simultaneously particle and wave ('wavicles'). Rather, they are neither particle nor wave but, in the appropriate circumstances, can behave like either. Capra has remarkably little to say about this phenomenon but it did inspire Gary Zukav to suggest that, 'We have little choice but to acknowledge that photons, which are energy, do appear to process information and to act accordingly, and that therefore, strange as it may sound, they seem to be organic'.[24] He seems to assume that all responses must be conscious responses!

Equally well-known is Heisenberg's Uncertainty Principle which asserts that it is impossible to measure both the position and momentum of a 'particle' to arbitrarily high degrees. Both this and wave-particle duality have serious implications for the Cartesian ideal of objectivity. Our choice of experiment plays a significant role in what can be measured. In other words we can no longer ignore observers: they have become participants.

But just what is the role of the observer? The Copenhagen interpretation of Niels Bohr and Max Born (two pioneers of quantum mechanics) certainly seems to favour the idealism of Capra and others. It suggests that quantum reality only becomes determinate when we measure it. Apparently physical reality does not exist independently of the observer and his equipment. This seems to give just what Capra wants: not only is reality-in-itself indeterminate (like his description of the One in eastern mysticism) but the observer plays a crucial role in creating determinate reality. We create our own reality or at least affect it in a very fundamental way by what we choose to observe. Thus he concludes that 'the structures and phenomena we observe in nature are nothing but creations of our measuring and categorizing mind'.[25]

What Capra omits to mention is that this interpretation is not entirely independent of his metaphysics. Niels Bohr took as his coat-of-arms the *T'ai-chi T'u* ('Diagram of the Supreme Ultimate': the Taoist symbol which depicts the archetypal opposites *Yin* and *Yang* in rotational symmetry) surmounted by the motto *contraria sunt complementa* (opposites are complementary). In so doing he was making a conscious connection between his pioneering work in quantum mechanics and Taoist metaphysics.

Furthermore this is by no means the only possible interpretation of quantum mechanics. At least five alternatives are seriously entertained by physicists.[26] Capra is building on shaky foundations when he relies upon one particular interpretation of quantum mechanics to support his point of view. As Christians have too often discovered, today's science has a bad habit of becoming yesterday's superstition: a faith which is too closely wedded to current scientific models runs the risk of rapidly being overtaken by new scientific developments. In fact, the sociologist Gordon Melton sees this as a major danger facing the New Age movement in the 1990s.[27]

Part II

Understanding the New Age

6

Beyond Reason:
Knowledge and Wisdom in the New Age

1. KNOWLEDGE IN THE OLD AGE

An important feature of the New Age phenomenon is its reaction against the dominant western view of knowledge, understanding, and wisdom. In order to understand that reaction, it would be helpful to survey the more traditional western views which form its context.

(a) The problem of knowledge

'How can I know this is so?' 'How can I be certain?' Questions of this kind have been a fundamental concern of western thinkers since ancient times. However they are also fraught with difficulties.

The question of certainty has had particular prominence. What is the basis which enables me to say that some assertion is reliable? Is there, indeed, a single universal basis for such assertions? How can I know whether '2 + 2 = 4', 'grass is green', and 'God loves me' are true? Issues of this kind have resulted in two competing traditions within western philosophy: *rationalism* and *empiricism*.

(b) Empiricism

The common sense approach to knowledge has always been to relate it to our five senses. We can trust assertions which we can confirm by observation. *Empiricists* believe that sense experience is a reliable source and basis for what we can know.

This approach places strict limits on what counts as knowledge. Much of the world in which we live is inaccessible to our five senses. The limits can be pushed back by measuring instruments such as microscopes, radio telescopes, X-ray machines, and geiger counters. Indeed empirical knowledge is closely associated with western science. Nevertheless vast tracts of human thought and experience remain inaccessible to our senses. These include the whole of mathematics; the experience of love, of beauty, and of goodness; and belief in God.

Empiricism also has the potential to be extremely subjective. This may not be immediately apparent because traditional British empiricism regarded the mind as a passive receptor for sense experience: everything we know is based upon experience, either directly or by subsequent reflection. However, it is *our* experience that matters: what *we* can see, hear, touch, taste, and smell. This was recognized by some of the earliest empirical philosophers, the Sophists of classical Greece. A leading Sophist, Protagoras, concluded that 'Man is the measure of all things.' In other words, 'whatever appears to any individual to be the case, including the report of his senses, must be so'.[1] But this is tantamount to a philosophical legitimation of credulity.

In order to avoid this difficulty, many empiricists have been driven to scepticism. Protagoras' contemporary and fellow Sophist, Gorgias, maintained that 'Nothing exists . . . If there were anything, then it could not be known. . . . Even if there were knowledge of being, this knowledge could not be imparted'.[2] A more recent example would be the radical Scottish empiricist, David Hume.

(c) Rationalism

Is there a more certain basis for knowledge than sense experience? Mathematical statements do not seem to be a matter of experience. But they appear to possess a necessity which empirical statements do not share. 'Grass is green' is generally true – but not universally true, as witness the state of my front lawn after another dry summer! $2 + 2 = 4$ is not in the same class: it is not conceivable that sometimes $2 + 2 = 5$.

With mathematics as his paradigm, one of the greatest philosophers of all times, Plato, set out to articulate an alternative to empiricism. He was familiar with the thought of Protagoras and hoped to demonstrate that there is a reality more certain than the ephemeral one disclosed by our senses. That reality was the realm of rational thought. For Plato, the reality of the external world was secondary to and derived from the reality of the realm of ideas. Thus he was prepared to recommend rational introspection as a more reliable source of knowledge than observation.

Rationalism has played an important part in the development of more recent philosophy thanks to the contribution of Descartes (a philosopher New Agers love to hate). Just how important reason was to Descartes is dramatically illustrated by his famous statement, '*Cogito, ergo sum*': 'I am thinking, therefore I exist.' No amount of observation could overcome his scepticism about his own existence. Only the for-him-indisputable fact of his own rational activity was sufficient assurance of his own existence.

In his *Meditations*, he proceeded from that basis to prove the existence of God and, thence, of physical reality. For Descartes, as for Plato and other rationalists, certainty was to be achieved by deductive reasoning from self-evident truths or innate ideas.

Descartes' rationalism, like Plato's, is closely associated with certain metaphysical assumptions. Both were mind-body dualists; they assumed that there are two realities – the rational or ideal, and the physical – and that the former takes priority over the latter.

(d) Kant's Copernican revolution in knowledge

Probably the single most important contribution to western philosophy in the past two hundred and fifty years is that of Immanuel Kant (1724–1804). As a young man he began to develop an elaborate speculative natural philosophy based on Newtonian physics. However his metaphysical pretensions were shattered by reading David Hume. The Scot's scepticism left him with an uneasy awareness of the limitations of empirical knowledge.

Subsequently he set himself the task of developing a critical philosophy in which he sought to bring together the best of empiricism and rationalism. The motto for his efforts might well have been, 'Reason without sense perception is empty. Sense perception without reason is blind.'

One of his most important contributions to the study of knowledge was his explicit recognition of the active role of the one who is doing the knowing. This 'turn to the subject' constituted a significant shift of perspective. No longer was the mind assumed to be the passive recipient of sense perceptions. On the contrary, in Kant's view, all sense perceptions are actively structured by the mind.

However, Kant's approach to knowledge, like empiricism, places severe limits on what can be known. Only the world of appearances is knowable. We have no access to reality-in-itself. This had at least two major implications. It meant that speculative cosmology on the basis of empirical findings was not a legitimate exercise. But neither was it legitimate to push beyond the limits by means of pure reason alone. This ruled out the search for rational arguments for the existence of God. It also made it impossible for philosophers to achieve a rational solution of the debate over free-will v. determinism.

(e) Knowledge after Kant

Subsequent epistemology has been marked by a succession of attempts to bridge the gap between the world of appearances and reality-in-itself.

A variety of philosophies have been developed in which the human mind is presented as the bridge between the two realms. For example, Hegel believed that reason *was* able to unite appearance and reality. This was because, for Hegel, the Absolute was self-thinking Thought.

Other philosophers, despairing of the possibility of uniting appearance and reality by means of reason, proposed human will as the bridge point. The most distinguished proponents of this approach were Schopenhauer and Nietzsche.

Yet another approach was the denial of 'reality-in-itself'. This led to the reassertion of radical empiricism in the form of Logical Positivism. Some members of this school took empiricism so far that they were prepared to reduce scientific theories to the level of convenient summaries of observations. Again this led to vast tracts of human experience being dismissed as literally meaningless. Amongst the areas treated in this way were love, morality, and religion.

The New Age offers one more way of bridging the gap: a new form of empiricism. But, in order to show that its epistemology is essentially empirical, we must begin by examining its critique of the western emphasis on reason.

2. THE DIVERSITY OF MENTAL PROCESSES

(a) The identification of the mind with reason

The history of western psychology has been closely linked with the way in which epistemology has developed. It would not be too much of an exaggeration to say that, by and large, western epistemology has focussed on the quest for reliable knowledge of the physical world. For the past three centuries scientific knowledge has been the paradigm for all knowledge.

Because of this emphasis, considerations of mental activity have, until recently, been dominated by an interest in rational thought. There has been a tendency to treat reason as the only legitimate mental activity.

Nor has theology been immune from this tendency. In western theology, personhood has tended to be defined in terms of rationality,[3] e.g., Boethius' definition: 'an individual substance of rational nature'. Admittedly, 'reason' had a much broader meaning when that was formulated. But western Christianity has tended to follow philosophical fashions in gradually narrowing its understanding of reason.

What became of other mental processes? Their existence was admitted but they were denied legitimacy. Where possible they were ignored. If they proved too persistent to ignore they were condemned as *ir*-rational. The word 'irrational' still possesses much of its condemnatory force today in spite of several generations of interest in the unconscious dimension of the mind. Within western Christianity this tendency is reflected by those theologians who equated the irrational, animal aspect of human nature with sinfulness.

This tendency is well illustrated by the dismissive attitude to dreams exhibited by those who place the highest value on rationality. For example, the Nobel prize-winning biochemist Francis Crick has dismissed dreaming as the dustbin of the brain. Similar sentiments may be found in the writings of the pioneer experimental psychologist, Wilhelm Wundt, who regarded dreams as a type of illusion. Perhaps most significant of all is the judgement of the father of western philosophy, Plato: he believed dreams to be the expression of the beast in man.

(b) The mind is more than reason

The effect of the West's obsession with reason has been the marginalization of much that goes on in our minds. It was not until the beginning of the twentieth century, and the pioneering work of Freud and Jung, that this tendency began to be questioned.

Nearly a century later those first tentative explorations of the unconscious have borne fruit in the contemporary questioning of this prejudice against the non-rational. Today many voices would echo Hamlet's 'There are more things in heaven and earth, Horatio, than are dreamt of in your philosophy.' The New Age movement is just one voice, albeit a particularly strident voice, in this trend.

New age questioning of the western identification of mind and reason, like so many aspects of the New Age, takes a variety of forms. Some New Agers have reacted against the West's emphasis on reason. They go to the other extreme, attempting to deny reason any legitimate place within New Age thought. For example, the New Age guru, Bhagwan Shree Rajneesh asserted, 'It is not that the intellect sometimes misunderstands. Rather, the intellect always misunderstands. It is not that the intellect sometimes errs; it is that the intellect is the error. It always errs'.[4]

Most New Agers do not go to such extremes. They prefer to present rational and non-rational mental processes as complementary. Both kinds of process are regarded as legitimate modes of knowing.

The most common way of expressing this complementarity is by means of Robert Ornstein's theory of hemispheres. In its original form this was a psychological theory based upon the behaviour of patients who had undergone major brain surgery. It was found that the two halves or hemispheres of the brain functioned autonomously and were responsible for different activities. For example, it was found that the right hemisphere of the brain controlled motion on the left side of the body and vice versa. It was also found that the left hemisphere controlled speech.

This theory has been generalized and is widely used by New Agers to relate psychological functions to hemisphere. Thus the articulate left hemisphere is regarded as the seat of our rational, analytical, systematizing powers. Conversely the inarticulate right hemisphere is the seat of our emotions, intuition, sexuality, and creativity.

Notice that the functions ascribed to the left hemisphere are those which in western society have been associated with the male, with culture, with all that is finest in us. The functions associated with the right hemisphere correspond to what western society has dismissed or condemned as feminine, irrational, or bestial.

The New Age's adoption of this theory represents an internalization of these dualisms. It implies that they can be transcended within the person by recognizing them as complementary rather than contradictory.

Their diagnosis of our society's problems is that we have relied too heavily on the very obvious powers of the left hemisphere. We have become obsessed with one aspect of the brain's functions at the expense of allowing other functions to atrophy. In order to overcome our personal and social crises we must seek ways of improving communication between the two hemispheres.

Left and right brain are complementary. Reason *and* emotion; analysis *and* intuition of the whole; ordinary *and* altered states of consciousness: we need them all if we are to function fully as human beings. That is the New Age ideal.

Thus Marilyn Ferguson calls for an exploration of techniques 'designed to reopen the bridge between right and left to through traffic, to increase the left brain's awareness of its counterpart', but she adds, 'Whatever lowers the barrier and lets the unclaimed material emerge is transformative. . . . Incantations, mantras, poetry, and secret sacred words are all bridges that join the two brains'.[5] Again we may well question the naivety with which all psychological, spiritual and occult disciplines are welcomed.

(c) Non-rational modes of 'knowing'

New Agers signal this insistence on the complementarity of rational and non-rational mental processes by describing both as modes of 'knowing'. Intuition, feeling and the myriad altered states of consciousness are all ways in which we know. One difficulty in attempting to describe these alternative modes of knowing is that New Agers do not agree about what such terms mean.

Intuition, for example, is used in many different ways. At its broadest, it does duty as a blanket term for all alternative modes of consciousness. Capra uses it like this: everything that does not pertain to reason is ascribed to intuition.[6] A more disciplined use of the term is adopted by those who have been influenced by the work of Jung. In his work on psychological types, Jung highlighted four psychological functions (sensing, intuition, thinking, and feeling) which could be clearly described and thus could form the basis of a reliable psychological typology. According to Jung, intuition is a mode of perception analogous to and complementary with sense perception. Far from being some esoteric hunch producing power, Jung understood intuition as the activity of the unconscious mind, taking the many insignificant sensory signals we normally overlook and processing them to see the overall pattern.

3. A NEW EMPIRICISM?

(a) The bridge between the worlds

Like Hegel, Schopenhauer and Nietzsche, the New Age proclaims that the human mind is capable of bridging the gap between appearance and reality.

However, its approach to reality-in-itself is very different from that of Hegel (or, for that matter, of earlier rationalists like Plato). It is an essentially empirical approach. New Agers claim that we have direct empirical access to both realms: to reality-in-itself as well as to the world of appearances.

They accept the common sense empirical view that sensory perception and the use of reason provide us with more or less reliable knowledge about the external world; the world of phenomena or appearances. But they assert that altered states of consciousness and other non-rational mental processes are also sources of empirical knowledge. The mind altering effects of drugs, or meditation, or the myriad of other psychotechnologies put us in direct touch with reality-in-itself.

Many suggest that modern physics, with its discovery of the non-pictureable nature of the sub-atomic realm, confirms what mystics have been saying for centuries. Thus Marilyn Ferguson claims that 'the discoveries of science have begun to make sense of mystical experiences people have been having for millenia. They suggest that we can tap into that order of reality *behind the world of appearances*'.[7]

Capra is even more explicit. He asserts that eastern mysticism is concerned with 'a direct experience of reality'.[8] But he insists that this experience is empirical. In fact, he draws extensive parallels between experimental science and eastern mysticism. Both are founded upon experience; both are repeatable. And he cites the Buddhist scholar D. T. Suzuki: 'Personal experience is . . . the foundation of Buddhist philosophy. In this sense Buddhism is radical empiricism or experientialism, whatever dialectic later developed to probe the meaning of enlightenment-experience'.[9]

In effect, New Agers claim that whatever we experience in

an altered state of consciousness must be regarded as real. It provides us with information about an inner reality (or reality-in-itself) which is no less reliable than our sense experience. Contemporary occultists take a very similar attitude. Thus Margot Adler comments on three very different approaches to occultism, 'they all seem to agree that Neo-Pagan magical systems are "maps" for learning about what appears to be an objective reality but often defies analysis.' And she describes this reality as a 'kind of psychic sea, from which a minority have been able to extract certain kinds of information'.[10]

Implicit in this is a belief that all mental activity is a valid source of knowledge, information, or wisdom. Every experience provides us with information about the worlds in which we live.

(b) The road to credulity

Radical empiricism is usually regarded as a high road to scepticism. It places all assertions about reality under a shadow of doubt.

Something of this can be seen in the epistemological work of Gregory Bateson. Bateson, although not himself a New Ager, has had a profound influence on American New Age approaches to knowledge because of his long association with Esalen.

Like New Agers he extended the concept of knowledge far beyond the content of rational activity. He even went as far as to suggest that evolution is a mental process. However, one of his favourite sayings was 'the map is not the territory'. The point of the saying is, of course, the Kantian one that the territory (reality-in-itself) is unknowable. We have to be content with our map-making activity and even that is dubious.

Such scepticism is sometimes displayed by members of the Pagan and New Age communities. However, more common is the alternative response to empiricism referred to above. For New Agers, as for Protagoras, man is the measure of all things. Scepticism is recast in an optimistic mode: if nothing is certain, then anything is possible. It is no less rational and certainly far more comforting to believe anything than it is to believe nothing.

The close relationship between scepticism and credulity is highlighted by the way both extremes may be found in the same individuals. Indeed Robert Anton Wilson claims that 'The most advance shamanic techniques . . . work by alternating faith and skepticism until you get beyond the ordinary limits of both'.[11]

(c) Pragmatism in the New Age

Anything goes; anything is believable. How then can a New Ager arrive at any decisions about what will be believed?

The New Age tendency to scepticism and/or credulity implies that questions of truth must be ruled out of court. Ideas need not correspond to any reality or even cohere with other ideas. Truth and falsehood are simply not useful concepts within a New Age perspective.

The New Age solution is uncannily like that of the Sophists: pragmatism. Since the truth of an idea cannot be established, what matters is its survival value. Does it satisfactorily express my experience? Does it help me cope with life? Most importantly, does it help me develop my full potential as a human being? The Sophists, like the New Agers, were renowned for their emphasis on training for success. Indeed 'sophistry' became a term of abuse precisely because some Sophists were prepared to teach techniques for winning arguments without regard for truth or morality. A similar comment might be made about some of the less scrupulous New Age management courses which promote manipulative techniques drawn from hypnotherapy.

An important implication of pragmatism is that it is inherently relativistic. If it works for me, it is 'true' for me. But it might not work for you. Therefore ideas and concepts can only be relatively true. They are necessarily limited, partial insights filtered through the particular experience and cultural background of each individual. This also applies in the realm of morality: a particular course of action may be moral for me but immoral for you. Some of the implications of this relativism will be explored in subsequent chapters.

The One and the Many:
Reality in the New Age

1. REALITY IS EVOLUTIONARY

(a) Evolution as a metaphysical principle

As I have already indicated, New Agers see evolution as more than a biological theory. In fact, it is one of the underlying assumptions governing New Age understandings of reality.

Thus, whatever their differences on other matters, virtually all New Agers would agree that we have to think of reality as 'in process'. When they accuse western thought of reductionism they often mean that it tends to present reality as made up of static, unchanging building blocks which may be arranged in different ways (the outlook of classical atomism). Rejecting such a view as too static, they see every entity as dynamic, changing, evolving, and relating to other entities in ways which also change over time. Not just living systems but the entire cosmos is characterized by this evolutionary dynamism.

(b) Cosmic evolution and mythology

However, with their shift away from the West's traditional stress on reason, New Agers demonstrate considerable dissatisfaction with unadorned metaphysical principles. One of the strengths of the New Age movement lies in its rediscovery of the power of story and myth.

Thus much of what the New Age has to say about evolution (and, indeed, its other beliefs) is couched in mythological terms. The role of evolution is presented through versions of Teilhard's cosmic evolutionary vision. Myths of the Earth Goddess are overhauled and presented as visions of planetary consciousness (the immediate goal of evolution).

This mythological presentation distinguishes New Age thinking from other contemporary evolutionary philosophies. This is more than a matter of style. It is one more sign of the New Age's departure from reason-dominated epistemologies.

Specifically it distinguishes New Age views on evolution from those of Process Philosophy. The latter originated with the work of the British mathematician and philosopher Alfred North Whitehead. Although Whitehead and his philosophical perspective are sometimes cited with approval by New Agers, they have little in common beyond a shared belief in the importance of evolution as a metaphysical principle.

(c) Progress in the New Age

One point at which New Agers depart from most evolutionary biologists is in their rejection of the notion that evolution is undirected. The New Age philosopher Ken Wilber made this clear when he commented that 'I really trust evolution. I really don't think God would screw us around that bad. God might be slow, but God's not dumb'.[1]

Individual steps in the evolutionary process may appear to be random. However, if you take a sufficiently large perspective, it is possible to discern a pattern amongst the random steps. There is a 'hidden hand' which guides the direction of evolution.

This view of evolution is closely related to the Enlightenment doctrine of progress which emerged as a secularization of the Christian doctrine of providence. Belief in a personal God, actively involved in creation, was replaced by belief in an active principle of harmony. For example, in the economic sphere, it was believed that the competitiveness and greed of individuals would cancel out to produce a just economic structure because of this underlying principle of harmony.

A similar view seems to prevail amongst New Agers. Their optimistic view of the future stems from their assurance that a 'hidden hand', cosmic harmony, or divine love will prevail in spite of human ignorance. What constitutes 'progress' has changed: spiritual awakening and planetary consciousness have replaced technological dominance and liberal democracy as the marks of progress. But faith in progress remains unshaken.

(d) Evolution of the New Age

Almost all New Agers believe that we are living through a critical stage in the evolution of the planet. The details of the transition are presented in very different ways. However, it is possible to subdivide New Age views about the future of the world into three classes.

(i) *Apocalypse soon*: Some New Agers believe the human race is set on an inevitable road to catastrophe. In view of the rapprochement between East and West, nuclear war seems less likely. However, a global environmental catastrophe is still seen as a distinct possibility. Such a catastrophe would destroy society as we know it and allow well-organized groups of survivors to impose their social structures on a global scale.

(ii) *Utopia soon*: A more common view is that the human race will be able to avoid the threatened catastrophe. Personal transformation through New Age techniques will affect a sufficiently large minority of the population to transform our social and economic structures, saving us from calamity. Humanity will create the New Age.

In fact the very forces which threaten us will be transformed into agents for our renewal. 'The crises of our time . . . are the necessary impetus for the revolution now under way . . . Our pathology is our opportunity.'[2]

(iii) *Transition as metaphor*: A minority of New Age intellectuals deny that the New Age is a literal historical event due to occur in the near future. For them it is a metaphor for personal transformation: by acting as if they were preparing for a new age, people are enabled to be more creative and compassionate. It enables New Agers to find the inner strength for self-actualization.

2. ALL THINGS ARE INTERCONNECTED

(a) The principle of interconnectedness·

Often labelled holism, this is a primary motivating factor behind such areas of New Age concern as holistic health and environmentalism. It undergirds the frequent assertion that mind, body, and spirit are so intimately interrelated as to be completely interdependent.

The principle asserts that everything is intimately related to everything else (in a non-hierarchical fashion).

For New Agers, interconnectedness is fundamental to being: 'I relate, therefore I exist.' Furthermore, every network of relationships is an entity in its own right. Thus they have no difficulty in envisaging the global ecosystem as a single living creature, Gaia. Taken to its logical conclusion, the entire cosmos may be envisaged as a single entity which in a very real sense is greater than the sum of its parts. Ultimately, all entities may be regarded as mutually interdependent elements of a single dynamic reality.

(b) Interconnectedness and evolution

How is this principle related to the equally important principle of evolution?

In Chapter 5 I traced the roots of evolution back to Hellenistic belief in the Great Chain of Being. The Principle of Interconnectedness stresses another aspect of this classical metaphysical scheme. The Great Chain was a single interrelated system. Interconnectedness revives that aspect while playing down the hierarchical nature of the relationships.

Members of the Green spirituality movement have adopted a non-hierarchical Principle of Interconnectedness to combat the popular connection between evolution and superiority. They stress our relatedness to other living beings while denying that we are superior. Thus interconnectedness functions as a check on the hierarchical tendencies of evolutionary thought. For Greens the Great Chain no longer hangs down from heaven to earth but has been tied in upon itself in countless ways – more of a Gordian knot than a chain.

However, other New Agers (particularly those influenced by theosophy and anthroposophy) have a more hierarchical understanding of interconnectedness. For example, the elder statesman of the New Age in Britain, Sir George Trevelyan, sees the natural world as a clear hierarchy, culminating in humankind: 'Man is the central purpose of it all. He appears as the great experiment of God'.[3] Indeed, he presents all other creatures as more or less bungled precursors of the human body; trial runs in the development of a body suitable for spiritual beings.[4]

(c) Holistic (or systems) thinking

The New Age's alternative to reductive analytical thought also stresses interconnectedness. Their approach to a problem focusses on its larger context. It reminds us that, in the real world, problems can never be completely isolated. The immediate solution to one problem may, in fact, cause greater problems elsewhere. The catalogue of environmental disasters which have resulted from well-meaning but narrowly conceived attempts to solve particular problems is ample proof of the value of systems thinking.

This is an important corrective to analysis. But questions must be asked when it is presented as a superior alternative to analytical thought. Holistic awareness without analysis to complement it is a recipe for impotence, e.g., viewing the environmental crisis in all its complexity may well leave us at a loss as to how we should respond. Control and manipulation are dirty words amongst New Agers but life in this world actually requires that we manipulate the world to some extent.

(d) Socio-political implications

The New Age often appears to be highly individualistic. Many critics have commented upon its apparent narcissism, its cult of the self.

It is true that New Agers are often anti-authoritarian and

that great emphasis is placed upon individual responsibility. But, at a deeper level, the Principle of Interconnectedness acts as a control on individualism by reminding its adherents that individuality is only relative. We are all interrelated; we cannot function, or even exist, in isolation from one another.

Thus the Principle of Interconnectedness favours the development of non-hierarchical social structures. This is precisely what we see amongst New Agers. The characteristic social structures of the New Age, communities and networks, are just what one would expect of attempts to apply interconnectedness to society.

However, unguarded application of this principle to human relationships may lead to the subordination of the individual to the whole. This is particularly true of its more hierarchical forms. When this happens, it is possible for true community to give way to an unacknowledged authoritarianism.

(e) Interconnectedness and pantheism

Christian critics of the New Age often identify interconnectedness with pantheism. There is certainly a close connection between the two. However, it is a misleading oversimplification merely to identify the one with the other.

In fact, it is perfectly possible for an atheist to adopt the Principle of Interconnectedness. There is nothing inherently religious about asserting that all entities are intimately interrelated. You can have holism without reverence.

However that does not apply to the New Age. Whatever else it may or may not be, the New Age is a spiritual perspective on life. But what should we revere or worship? And how might the Principle of Interconnectedness influence our choice of religious belief?

Clearly belief in interconnectedness rules out *deism*. This is the belief that a transcendent deity created the universe and subsequently left it to its own devices. Such a god is completely unrelated to the world and, therefore, anathema to anyone who believes that all entities are interrelated.

What about *theism*: belief in a god who has a continuing (personal) relationship with the universe? The Principle of

Interconnectedness does not rule out belief in one or more personal deities. However, it may relativize theism, by insisting that those deities be seen as part of a greater whole. Taken as a fundamental guiding principle, interconnectedness undermines the fundamental distinction between creator and creation which is an essential feature of the Christian doctrine of God.

This does not mean that Christianity and belief in interconnectedness are mutually exclusive. On the contrary it can be argued that a biblical view of creation includes interconnectedness as one of its characteristics. This is not an arbitrary limitation of interconnectedness intended to safeguard the transcendence of God. Rather it sees interconnectedness as the creaturely reflection of the interrelatedness which is fundamental to the Christian understanding of God as Trinity.

There is one remaining option. If all things, spiritual and material, are inextricably linked together to form a Whole, that Whole is the most inclusive and satisfying object of worship. When combined with a spiritual outlook and freed from the constraints of orthodox Christian doctrine, interconnectedness does indeed result in *pantheism*.

Thus pantheistic sentiments are to be found in a wide range of New Age literature. For example, Fritjof Capra defines God as 'the self-organizing dynamics of the entire cosmos'.[5] Similarly Marilyn Ferguson speaks of God as 'the consciousness that manifests as . . . the play of the universe. God is the organizing matrix we can experience but not tell, that which enlivens matter'.[6]

Many people have been attracted to pantheism because they see in it a way of transforming our attitude to the environment and, thus, averting environmental catastrophe. They argue that only by rediscovering reverence for the earth can we hope to build a stable relationship with the natural world. The biologist Rupert Sheldrake sees this as the way 'to develop a richer understanding of human nature, shaped by tradition and collective memory; linked to the Earth and the heavens, related to all forms of life; and consciously open to the creative power expressed in all evolution'.[7]

Ironically, far from promoting environmental responsibility, pantheism may actually undermine it. Investing the cosmos with divine attributes may be a recipe for denying that human beings have the power to damage the global ecosystem. This tendency is further reinforced by Jim Lovelock's insistence on the resilience of Gaia. Thus Elisabet Sahtouris asserts that 'we are wrong to devote our attention to saving or managing nature. Gaia will save herself – with or without us – and hardly needs advice or help in management'.[8] Similarly Sir George Trevelyan is confident that 'Ultimately Gaia is undefeatable, since her intelligence can compel any part of her organism to come into harmony with her whole structure'.[9]

From a Christian perspective, pantheistic spirituality appears unsatisfactory because it leaves little room for personhood. Human beings are islands of subjectivity in a basically impersonal cosmos and many of the techniques of pantheistic spirituality appear to be designed to suppress my individual self-consciousness in favour of closer identification with the Whole.

3. THE ONE AND THE MANY

New Agers discern two realms of experience; two aspects or dimensions of reality. They are by no means the first people to have noticed this duality. On the contrary, it underlies one of the most ancient riddles of philosophy. How are we to relate the One and the Many?

(a) The Many

For New Agers experience is a primary determinant of what is real. Thus they take seriously the realm of sense experience. The chief characteristic of this realm is its multiplicity; it is the realm of the Many.

One of the attractive features of worship amongst New Agers and Neo-Pagans is their apparent capacity to affirm and celebrate this aspect of reality. All the senses are engaged and focussed in acts of ritual worship.

(b) The One

At the same time, through altered states of consciousness, New Agers believe they have direct access to another dimension of reality. This inner reality is often identified with Kant's concept of reality-in-itself.

Perhaps one of the most significant titles for it is the one popularized by Aldous Huxley. He spoke of this realm as 'Mind at Large'. In doing so he identified the two realms with the duality which Descartes sharpened into a dualism of mind and matter.

The experienced content of this realm is incredibly diverse. For example, Marilyn Ferguson summarizes experience of inner reality in the following terms:

> Loss of ego boundaries and the sudden identification with all of life (a melting into the universe); lights; altered color perception; thrills; electrical sensations; sense of expanding like a bubble or bounding upward; banishment of fear, particularly fear of death; roaring sound; wind; feeling of being separated from physical self; bliss; sharp awareness of patterns; a sense of liberation; a blending of the senses (synesthesia), as when colors are heard and sights produce auditory sensations; an oceanic feeling; a belief that one has awakened; that the experience is the only reality and that ordinary consciousness is but its poor shadow; and a sense of transcending time and space.[10]

But, in spite of its diversity, a recurring feature of this cosmic consciousness is its unitary nature. It stands in sharp contrast to the multiplicity of the world of the physical senses. Common to this state is a direct experience of the wholeness of the cosmos. Not only is it experienced as a single entity but the experiencing self is often identified with that entity. This is close to the fundamental tenet of Hinduism that *Atman* (the individual self) is *Brahman* (the cosmic self).

(c) Relating the One and the Many

Basically there are four ways in which we might attempt to relate the One and the Many; mind and matter. The first is to deny that they can be related. We may follow the lead of Descartes and treat mind and matter as co-equal but entirely independent realities. This is the path of metaphysical *dualism*. However, it is not an option open to New Agers. It is excluded by their insistence on the interconnectedness of all things, including mind and matter.

That leaves three options open to New Agers. They may treat one realm as the cause of the other. This creates two options depending on which is given priority: *monism* (the One is prior to the Many) and what has been called the *psychedelic* option[11] (the experience of unity is a product of the Many). The third option is to treat the two realms as co-equal but mutually interdependent (the One cannot exist without the Many, nor the Many without the One). I call this the *pluralistic* option to distinguish it from both monism and dualism.

4. PSYCHEDELIC REALITIES

(a) The priority of the Many

Since it is readily accommodated to materialist understandings of the relationship between matter and mind, this is the least radical option open to New Agers.

Materialism treats the material world (the Many) as primary reality. Any other aspect of reality is explained as a product or function of material entities as they interact with one another. Thus, for the materialist, the concepts of mind and spirit are acceptable only if they are understood entirely as the products of interactions within complex configurations of matter.

Traditionally this leads to a strongly reductionist view of mental activity. It is the philosophy underlying behaviourist psychology: an approach which denies that mental activity is accessible to scientific investigation (by implication, at least, questioning its reality) and insists that to be scientific psychology must restrict itself to the study of visible human behaviour. Thus, 'To find that most people have minds . . . is simply to find that they are able and prone to do certain things.'[12]

However, it is possible to reconcile materialism and holism. Thus, while maintaining that all phenomena can be explained in terms of material interactions, some materialists would maintain that the systems of interacting particles are interesting in their own right.

(b) The nature of psychedelic reality

The psychedelic view of inner reality portrays it as the product of mental activity. Inner reality is something generated by the mind rather than another dimension to which the mind gains access. Ultimately the experiences described by Marilyn Ferguson are determined by the physiological and chemical state of the brain. The use of the term *psychedelic* reminds us both that this interpretation presents the mind or psyche as the cause of the experience and that it is closely associated with the widespread experimentation with hallucinogenic drugs in the 1960s. As James Sire comments, 'One does not so much open doors of perception as create a new reality to perceive'.[13]

It is tempting to dismiss this approach as mere subjectivism. However, from the perspective of its advocates, subjective reality is at least as important as objective reality.

They may defend their position by questioning our use of the labels 'subjective' and 'objective'. How objective are our sense impressions? Since the Enlightenment it has been widely agreed that we do not have direct access to objective sense impressions. They are all filtered through and interpreted by parts of the brain of which we are not normally conscious. Thus they too possess a degree of subjectivity. Even amongst scientists it is now widely agreed that 'there are no uninterpreted facts'.[14]

The psychedelic interpretation of inner reality is usually accompanied by an extreme version of this view: we have no access to objective reality but only to our interpretations of it. Thus altered states of consciousness are no less valid than normal consciousness and such experiences show that we possess some degree of freedom in how we choose to experience the world. Within certain limits (which are usually left undefined) we create our own realities.

(c) Mysticism as escapism

This approach promises that we can reshape our world by altering how we view it. To those who feel battered by the harsh reality of late twentieth-century western industrial society it offers the tempting possibility of escape. It suggests that by emigrating inwards we can experience the world differently.

Such promises make New Age management courses seem very attractive. They promise to transform the way you feel about your work, that by changing your attitude you can change your experience. And, within certain limits, this is true and such courses actually bring some degree of benefit.

However problems may arise because the limits have not been defined. How far can you go in reconstructing the world before your inner model ceases to bear any relation to outer reality? At what point do your mental constructs become so dissociated from outer reality that you have made the transition from sanity to schizophrenia?

5. NEW AGE MONISM

(a) The priority of the One

The monistic interpretation begins with Mind at Large, which it understands as the direct experience of ultimate reality. Thus what we experience as Inner Reality is reality-in-itself. It is logically and causally prior to the world of sense impressions.

For historical reasons this is the most popular New Age interpretation of reality. However, it is arguable that monism is not easily reconciled with the two metaphysical principles already identified in this chapter.

(b) Transcending multiplicity

According to monism ultimate reality is One. It is beyond distinction. It transcends even the distinction between subject and object which is fundamental to ordinary consciousness.

But how is this primordial unity to be related to our experience of the world in all its manifold complexity? The answer most accessible to the western mind is by means of the Great Chain of Being. At the top of the pyramid is the One, ultimate reality beyond all distinctions. The closer to the top of the pyramid, the more real an entity is. Reality is a function of closeness to ultimate unity. Conscious entities are closer to unity than unconscious ones: humans are 'higher' than mice, cabbages, or grains of sand.

Conversely, the more fragmented, the further from unity entities are, the less real they are. Thus the monist will argue that the complexity of the world is an illusion. What is real is our oneness.

And because it is illusory, multiplicity is, in itself, also meaningless. Mythological explanations about the origins of the illusory complexity we call the world underline its meaninglessness. It is presented as the play, the dream, or even the madness of the One/God.

The goal of a monistic cosmos is clear: the Many are gradually struggling back towards unification in the One. Thus the universe in all its diversity is seen not merely as meaningless but as evil. It is not fashionable in this environmentally conscious age to make such statements. Nevertheless, negative judgements about the material world do creep into the language of monistic New Agers. Thus 'the outer world is so cruel, so dangerous, so altogether ugly in many of its aspects that we are fully justified in turning inwards to discover the magic gateway into the greater spiritual realms'.[15] Significantly, the imagery of the Fall is often used to describe our present existence in a world of multiplicity.[16]

Clearly a consistent monistic philosophy is a very tenuous basis for environmentalism. Fundamental to practical environmental responsibility is a concern for diversity. The health of an ecosystem is closely related to its diversity. But in seeking to maintain and promote diversity, environmentalists are setting themselves against the fundamental thrust of cosmic evolution as understood by monists. It is true that environmental concern has emerged within contemporary Indian society[17] but the environmental track record of monistic cultures is by no means as enviable as some western Greens make out.[18]

More generally, monism undermines the Principle of Interconnectedness. While maintaining that all things are interconnected, it devalues the individual entities that make up the whole. Ultimately what matters is not an interconnected complex of entities but the undifferentiated One.

(c) Transcending time

According to monism, time and process are inextricably bound up with the experience of multiplicity. The One does not suffer change. It transcends time, occupying atemporal eternity. Therefore time, like multiplicity, is ultimately meaningless.

The meaninglessness of time is enshrined in the doctrine of eternal recurrence. In Indian mythology this is often portrayed as a cycle of cosmic ages; a concept often misread by New Agers as supporting their belief in astrological ages. However, there is no progress over these cycles. Whatever progress is made by humankind is blotted out at the end of the *Kali Yuga* (the age of destruction) leaving us to begin again in the next cycle. Alternatively, the relationship between the One and the Many may be presented in cyclical terms: the One loses itself/ falls into multiplicity, gradually struggles back to unity, only to fall again, and so on *ad infinitum*.

But what does this do to the principle of evolution? When the concept is used in a monistic context it must cease to have any historical or temporal reference. In effect it reverts to the classical metaphysics of the Great Chain of Being. Evolution is no longer about the origin and maintenance of biological diversity but about the ascent of spirit to unity.

(d) Transcending morality

If time and multiplicity are meaningless, then all action is meaningless. Indeed all action is counterproductive: it merely serves to reinforce individuality and multiplicity. Thus any action, whether good or bad, binds us more closely to the wheel of karma, to the law of cause and effect.

This has been given an ethical veneer by theosophy and its New Age derivatives. Moral action is seen as a step in the right direction: a moral person is closer to the One than an immoral person. But, although it may help us along the path, moral action will in the end prevent us from attaining the goal of reunification with the One. Eventually we must progress beyond moral action to *in*action. Thus consistent monism runs counter to the very real moral sensibilities displayed by many New Agers.

(e) Transcending personality

Since the One transcends even the fundamental split between subject and object, it transcends self-consciousness. The key to enlightenment is experiencing *Atman* (the individual self) as *Brahman* (the One).

As long as we remain self-aware, as long as we know ourselves to be experiencing subjects, we remain alienated from the One. Thus the goal of monism is the loss (or transcendence) of personal identity in the One.

A corollary of the loss of personal identity is the transcendence of personal relatedness. There can be no relationships within the One because relationship entails an other with whom one relates. Nor can there be any knowledge since there is nothing to know.

It would be a mistake to call the state of Oneness solipsistic. Solipsism demands self-awareness. The One cannot be self-aware without ceasing to be the One. It is only in the state of multiplicity that we can be aware of unity. I find myself asking how union with the One differs from annihilation.

6. NEW AGE PLURALISM

(a) More implications of interconnectedness

If the Principle of Interconnectedness is allowed to determine the answer to the question of how the One and the Many are related we arrive at a third option for New Agers. This is the view that the two aspects of reality are mutually interdependent with neither taking priority.

I have called this the *pluralistic* option because, although it maintains the reality and even divinity of the One, it refuses to deny the reality of the Many:

> All things are one, yet each is separate, individual, unique . . . The world of separate things is the reflection of the One, the One is the reflection of the myriad separate things of the world. We are all 'swirls' of the same energy, yet each swirl is unique in its own form and pattern.[19]

A musical analogy may be helpful in understanding this. Consider a Mozart symphony: it is a single work of art. But it consists of many notes, melodies, and harmonies. Which is more important? Which has priority? The work as a whole or its component parts? The question is unanswerable. The symphony cannot exist apart from the notes which make it up. Conversely the notes have no meaning apart from their location in the symphony.

Furthermore, a piece of music is a unity which unfolds over time. Thus it suggests a very different concept of unity to that adopted by monism. It would be incorrect to say that the music evolves since the development of the composition is part of the overall vision of the composer. Nevertheless, it indicates the possibility of maintaining a recognizable concept of evolution alongside a metaphysics of interconnectedness.

A pantheism which acknowledges the uniqueness of each component part of the whole is in a much stronger position to address the environmental crisis than one which denies their reality. It is able to recognize the importance for the harmonious functioning of the Whole of each entity. Thus each creature comes to be seen as being of equal value. The result is an ethic which accords equal rights to the land and its life forms. It leads to a lifestyle which has been summed up in the slogan 'living lightly on the land'.

(b) Interpreting inner reality

In view of this pluralistic option, what are we to make of experiences of psychic/unconscious reality? How shall we interpret the content of such experiences?

(i) *Literalism*: An interpretative option not open to the monist is literalism. The pluralist is free to take psychic experiences at their face value. Thus encounters with spirit guides may be accepted as such. Even John Lilly, one of the chief proponents of the psychedelic interpretation, sees this as a serious possibility.[20]

This approach dovetails into the many forms of occultism currently enjoying a revival in the West. Pluralistic, rather than monistic, pantheism is a recurring feature of western occultism.

(ii) *Symbolism*: Alternatively the contents of mystical experience may be given a metaphorical or symbolic interpretation. This is the approach adopted by depth psychology. Jung, for example, encountered spirit guides in his explorations of the psyche. He interpreted them not as real spiritual beings but as conscious manifestations of aspects of the unconscious.[21]

It should be noted that the two avenues of interpretation, symbolism and literalism, are not mutually exclusive. Many occultists are quite happy to interpret their experiences in both ways.

(c) Concluding comments

Pluralistic pantheism seems to me to be more consistent with the aspirations of ordinary New Agers than does its monistic alternative. This may partly explain why there appears to be a shift within the British New Age scene away from eastern mysticism and towards western occultism.[22]

Again, from a Christian perspective, the difficulties with this outlook lie not in pluralism as such but in its alliance with pantheism. Pantheism and orthodox Christianity are mutually exclusive. On the other hand, the Christian doctrine of creation is a pluralistic doctrine of creation: it portrays the material world as manifold but, at the same time, a single work of art.

8

Sages and Supermen:
New Age Visions of Humanity

1. THE IMPORTANCE OF ANTHROPOLOGY

> When I look at thy heavens, the work of thy fingers;
>   the moon and the stars which thou hast established;
> what is man that thou art mindful of him,
>   and the son of man that thou dost care for him?
>
> (Ps. 8:3,4)

What is man? Who am I? Every philosophical (or theological) system worthy of attention must address itself to such questions sooner or later. The answers to such questions constitute a philosophical anthropology. Every world-view has such an anthropology (and, in some cases, more than one).

Questions about the reality of human life, about who and what we are, may not be as fundamental as the questions of metaphysics. Nevertheless they are crucial, for our answers to such questions are the basis on which we make (or refuse to make) connections between reality and human existence. Thus they are fundamental to our ethical perspective: our expectations of human behaviour are inextricably bound up with what we understand humans to be.

2. THE STILL POINT OF THE TURNING WORLD

(a) Materialism rejected

The materialistic answer to the question 'what is man?' may be summed up very simply.

The human race is no more than a successful biological accident. The concepts of meaning and value have a role within the closed system of human culture. However, as soon as culture is placed in the larger context of physical reality meaning and value vanish. For the materialist the cosmos is meaningless and the human race is nothing more than a particularly successful animal species. The German philosopher Feuerbach underlined this in a characteristically pithy sentence: *Der Mensch ist, was er isst*; man is what he eats.

New Agers find this answer profoundly dissatisfying. Like Christians, they believe that human existence has meaning, that there is more to life than biology.

(b) The New Age answer

New Agers believe that human beings are in the crucial position of being the point of unity between the realm of appearances and reality-in-itself (or Mind at Large). We are matter become self-aware.

New Age thinking tends towards pantheism: it ascribes divinity to all things. But many New Agers also retain a hierarchical view of reality: all things may be divine, but some are more divine than others. If, in essence, the universe is a great thought, mind is closer to ultimate reality than matter. Conscious matter is a step up the hierarchy from unconscious matter. Thus, while granting the divinity of the non-human world, much New Age thought actually focusses on the divinity of humankind.

The world turns and turns, dancing meaninglessly in space. It is only within the human spirit that stillness and hence meaning is found. Someone once described Jesus Christ as 'the still point of the turning world' and in orthodox Christian theology he is often described as the *Logos*, the universe's ground of meaning and reason. New Age anthropology suggests that this can be true of every human being.

(c) Creating our own realities

We give the world its meaning. The New Age agrees with materialism in locating meaning and value within the realm of human subjectivity rather than physical objectivity. But thereafter it goes in a very different direction, grounding the material and the objective upon the subjective and the spiritual.

We give the world its meaning. This effectively means that, in some sense, we are its creators. But New Agers differ over the extent to which we create reality. Generally speaking, those who tend towards monism take this point much further than those whose view of reality is more pluralistic.

Thus the former might identify with the following sentiments:

> if we are in essence God, then the point is that we are free, really free, with the whole universe as our playground. Earth is not just a training ground for some life hereafter; it is an integral part of our eternal existence. The universe is ours to do in as we want. The universe is not static. It is not a succession of obstacle courses to be negotiated, with our reward an eternity of rest in some heavenly realm. The universe is our play. It is our creation, because ultimately we ourselves are God. In the universe, we are constantly setting ourselves new challenges, devising new games, and having more and more outrageous adventures.[1]

By contrast, pluralistic New Agers may well find such comments profoundly embarrassing and even dismiss them as megalomaniac. They will be more comfortable with a more balanced interplay between consciousness and reality: 'Consciousness shapes reality; reality shapes consciousness'.[2]

But how does consciousness shape reality? Starhawk defines magic as 'the art of changing consciousness at will'.[3] David Spangler's description of creative visualization points in the same direction:

> When you project an idea of something you would like, it takes shape and form . . . according to the power and clarity of your thought and desire. As you accept the reality of this unseen form, it takes on life and will precipitate itself into physical form.[4]

We can alter physical reality by will and imagination. Modern occultists even suggest that they create the gods and goddesses they worship. For example Starhawk asserts that the Goddess 'exists, *and* we create Her'.[5] This may sound self-contradictory but there is a rationale behind it: the Goddess is a projection. However, in contrast to nineteenth-century projection theories of religion, modern occultism sees such projections as a source of psychic power.

(d) Total responsibility

If we possess divine powers of creativity, we also bear divine responsibility for what happens in our worlds. New Agers often describe this as an ethic of total responsibility. There are no circumstances beyond my control; I am totally responsible for the reality I experience.

This has certain superficial attractions. After all, one of the most common excuses for human evil is 'I was just following orders.' From a New Age perspective that excuse is never legitimate: the concentration camp guard must be regarded as a co-creator of the system which killed six million Jews.

On the other hand, an ethic of total responsibility also implies that each of those six million Jews was also responsible for the system. New Agers sometimes speak of two kinds of consciousness: victim-consciousness and victor-consciousness. Part of what it means to fulfil your full human potential is to transform your own consciousness – to give up being a victim and choose to become a victor.

Such an outlook is potentially very dangerous. For example, the leaders of a New Age gathering in Wales used it to justify an anti-Semitic attack on one of the participants:

> They approached the woman who had been attacked, . . . 'We all create our own reality,' they told her. 'You have created this yourself, it's obviously part of your karma, but we really wish you hadn't manifested it on our field.' Then followed a patient lecture on 'victim consciousness,' and an invitation to leave the camp. Finally, the woman was told that if she chose to stay for the remaining two days, she

must promise not to speak to anyone else about what had happened. . . .

Later the woman asked another of the leading lights . . . 'This "victim-consciousness" thing. Do you think, then, that the Native American Indians were responsible for the genocide they suffered? . . . And that the people of Hiroshima and Nagasaki created their own deaths and mutilation by their own bad karma?'

The answer was 'Well yes. Ultimately, yes, the victims were responsible.'[6]

This should not be taken as evidence that New Age thought is generally anti-Semitic. There are affinities between some forms of New Age thought and Nazi ideology. But most New Agers would be quick to repudiate anti-Semitism and, indeed, any form of racism. However, this emphasis on victim-consciousness clearly undermines concern for social justice and resistance to oppression.

The victim-victor duality is symptomatic of a failure to take evil and suffering seriously enough. For example, Sir George Trevelyan recently warned of possible earthquakes, tidal waves and natural disasters in the years ahead. He then went on to say, 'a great many people will lose their bodies in the coming years . . . So what? . . . Death is nothing but the release from the necessary limitations of a soul embodied upon a natural earth'.[7] In a similar vein Ash and Hewitt suggest that 'Earth is an adventure playground where we can't really hurt ourselves, since even physical death cannot harm us'.[8]

In the end total responsibility may be indistinguishable from total irresponsibility – in the sense that nothing in this world is taken seriously. The AIDS pandemic, third-world famine and genocide are games we play.

(e) The paths to godhead

New Age anthropology elevates human beings to divinity: we are 'gods in the making . . . ultimately we ourselves are God'.[9] But there is no single New Age path to divinity. The ethic of total responsibility applies also to our spiritual pilgrimage: we are each responsible for finding our own path. Thus, in a sense there are as many paths as there are New Agers.

Within this diversity it is possible to discern different models of the path to godhood, suited to different temperaments. Some are more contemplative, others more active: some take the way of the sage, others that of the superman.

3. THE WISDOM OF THE SAGE

The way of the sage is the way of wisdom. By implication such a route to divinity is essentially élitist – only a select few have the mental and spiritual resources to find the way. It is hardly surprising that whenever the occult perspective has dominated a mass religion it has tended to encourage belief in reincarnation (it may take the average peasant millions of lives to achieve the level of spiritual development to be found in the élite).

The New Age sage differs from the occult sage at this point only in that he sees an alternative to the long slow process of spiritual evolution by reincarnation. Many New Age personal development courses suggest that the sought-for wisdom exists within every one of us (locked up in our unconscious or in the right hemisphere of the brain – the seat of intuition). Those courses may be regarded as shock tactics for gaining access to that information. As you might expect, many members of the traditional occult élite take a dim view of this, and are often very vocal in expressing their contempt for New Agers.

The way of the sage has a long and honourable history in western culture. It has taken many forms of which the following are merely examples.

(a) The Epicurean sage

It may seem strange to begin with Epicurus, a noted atheist, but it shows that atheism is no bar to occultism. On the contrary, atheism is quite consistent with the belief that the universe is essentially meaningless (and what are gods, if not meaning-makers?). In fact, one leading American occultist describes himself as a transcendental atheist, and atheism is a fundamental tenet of Anton LaVey's Church of Satan.

Technically Epicurus did not deny the existence of the gods but, like Buddha, he regarded them as finite beings trapped within the cosmic meaninglessness just as we are. The subversive nature of his philosophy led him to take steps to protect his followers from persecution. Specifically, he advised that the core of their doctrine be kept secret and that, in public, they should affirm the consensus faith.

Thus the Epicurean pursuit of wisdom entailed a twofold withdrawal from the world. There was the withdrawal to avoid hostile scrutiny. But their acceptance of ultimate meaninglessness also called for intellectual withdrawal. For the Epicureans intelligence had no more meaning than any other instinctive or reflex action. Thomas Molnar summarizes their response thus,

> after the sages have satisfied their intellectual curiosity, the best strategy for them is . . . to cultivate, undisturbed, their gardens and minds. They do not become gods because there are none; but by doing what the universe is doing they are as close to the status of pure inquiring intellect as it is possible to be. And in a godless universe, *this* is the supreme status.[10]

(b) The Stoic sage

Stoicism offered a more fully developed metaphysics and with it a more rounded morality than Epicureanism. In fact, so close was Stoic morality to Christian morality that it has tempted Christians for centuries. The Stoic ideal was to live life without being affected in any way by it: an attitude easily confused with certain interpretations of 'Do not love the world or the things in the world' (1 John 2:15).

But there again is the hint that Stoicism takes an entirely negative view of this life. It expects the worst and presents its most attractive face precisely at the moment the sage is confronting catastrophe. Again, because of its negative attitude to life, it teaches that in circumstances which preclude the maintenance of this quiet dignity it is more noble to commit suicide.

Our conscious existence in this life is a temporary state to be accepted with resignation. Death is a release into the universal fire which is the deity permeating all things.

(c) The Hermetic sage

The Hermeticists took their name from a collection of late pagan religio-philosophical treatises ascribed to Hermes Trismegistus, which were translated by Marsilio Ficino in the fifteenth century. The material represents a synthesis of Stoicism and Neoplatonism together with elements from eastern mysticism (probably mediated through one of the forms of Gnosticism). Those texts form the very heart of western occultism.

And the picture of the Hermetic sage is not very different from those we have already painted. A modern summary of Hermetic magic states that, 'The divine fragment is that part of us which is always seeking reunion, a reassembly of separated parts into the whole from which they were created; a return to the paradisial state before the Fall.'[11]

That is the goal of the sage – the overcoming of a Fall which is seen not as disobedience but as multiplicity. To be a finite creature is to be fallen. To save ourselves we must reunite ourselves with the One. This is so important that the writer later says, 'To look at the magician without taking into account his dream of unity, however partial or superficial, with deity, is to mistake his whole purpose'.[12]

This world is meaningless, an illusion of multiplicity generated in eternal silence. Man contains a tiny fragment of the divine light which seeks escape from its prison. The esoteric wisdom of the occultist is seen as a way of escape. By realizing what they really are the select few may be reunited with the divine.

4. THE WILL OF THE SUPERMAN

In many ways Friedrich Nietzsche may be regarded as an unacknowledged prophet of the New Age movement. Many of his ideas have been mediated to the New Age movement through the work of the Nobel Prize winning novelist Hermann Hesse.

Hesse's novels had a powerful impact on the development of the Counter Culture of the 1960s and 1970s. One of his biographers suggests that for many in the Counter Culture, 'he became a myth – a mixture of Jesus and Buddha in no way tied to contemporary time schedules or geography' and that the novels became 'pretexts for self-exploration'.[13] Hesse clearly regarded himself as a disciple of Nietzsche, immersing himself in Nietzsche's writings and even modelling his behaviour on that of Michel (the Nietzsche character in André Gide's novel, *The Immoralist*).

(a) The death of God

'God is dead.' Those three words of Nietzsche became the slogan of an entire school of liberal theology.

God is dead: man has come of age, he no longer needs the metaphor of a transcendent personal creator God. Unlike many of his readers, Nietzsche saw clearly the enormity of what this implied – that is why he put it in the form of an indictment: 'God is dead. . . . And we have killed him.'

Who has killed God? Nietzsche's audience was the secular intelligentsia of nineteenth-century Germany, confident that it was the very pinnacle of the Age of Reason. It had no need for such childish notions as 'God'. And Nietzsche threw this challenge in their face: our philosophy has killed God, but dare we face the implications of what we have done?

(b) The critique of morals

For post-Enlightenment philosophy, God was not so much untrue as irrelevant. God had been written out of their perspective as far as creation was concerned: they had their own naturalistic myths of creation. And redemption was superstitious nonsense: why should the cosmic watchmaker take a personal interest in insignificant creatures such as man when he was, in any case, clearly progressing towards perfection? But there was one point at which the Enlightenment retained a niche for God: it retained a belief in a transcendent ground of value and meaning.

Nietzsche would have none of this. His talk about the death of God was a dramatic way of making people face the fact that if, as the dominant philosophy implied, God did not exist, then we are bound not to transfer our worship to a hypothetical ground of goodness, truth, and beauty. He saw clearly that secularism cuts away the foundations of any objective morality, knowledge, and aesthetics. The death of God symbolizes the loss of all absolutes, all ultimates, all reference points. Nietzsche makes the point in characteristically rhetorical fashion:

'Where has God gone?' he cried. 'I shall tell you. *We have killed him* – you and I. We are all his murderers. But how have we done this? How were we able to drink up the sea? Who gave us the sponge to wipe away the entire horizon? What did we do when we unchained this earth from its sun? Whither is it moving now? Whither are we moving now? Away from all suns? Are we not perpetually falling? Backward, sideward, forward, in all directions? Is there any up or down left? Are we not straying as through an infinite nothing?[14]

Optimistic humanists sought a basis for morality in evolution. Nietzsche was frankly contemptuous of their efforts. If we have evolved, then why not our understanding of truth, beauty, and goodness? We are left without objective reference points.

What then are we to make of the very human obsession with morality? For Nietzsche the good, as commonly understood, was that which is useful for the existence, survival, and welfare of the community. In the prehistory of human community this was achieved by compulsion. But gradually the compulsion was interiorized to tradition and conscience. This sounds like utilitarianism – and it is. But Nietzsche went on to ask about the origin of that compulsion. He saw two possible sources.

One of these sources is the mass of humanity, the proletariat, or, as he preferred to call them, the herd. Nietzsche proposed a doctrine of resentment which is a remarkable negative image of Marx's doctrine of ideology. Marx regarded the notions of liberal democracy and religion (particularly Christianity) as the propaganda of a ruling élite, designed to keep the proletariat disinherited. For Nietzsche, those same ideas were spawned by the masses of ordinary humanity out of resentment. They were designed not so much to keep the proletariat content with their lot as to clip the wings of those heroic spirits who dared to soar above the common herd. The result is a slave morality which extols sympathy, kindness, and humility while denigrating strength and independence. It protects the interests of the herd at the expense of the individual and, by implication, is a dehumanizing force. Nietzsche regarded Christianity (together with its secular derivatives, liberalism and socialism) as the prime example of a slave morality.

Hesse's early novel *Unterrm Rad* demonstrates the effects of slave morality in education. It is an indictment of the German educational system in the nineteenth century. Hesse drew on his own experiences to show how mass education and the associated morality moulded the individual to fit society's expectations rather than allowing the individual to pursue his or her own potential. In Hesse's story, the hero is destroyed both mentally and physically by the resentment of the establishment.

The other possible source of the compulsion which leads to morality is the outstanding individual, the hero, the strong man, *der Führer*. In such a morality, power is good. Virtue understood as power was the basis of Hellenistic civilization and Nietzsche spoke admiringly of its manifestation in classical philosophy: 'These philosophers possessed a firm belief in themselves and their "truth" and with it they overthrew all their contemporaries and predecessors; each of them was a warlike brutal tyrant'.[15] The powerful man creates his own values and imposes them on the herd.

There are no equals in this morality, only rivals. By implication it admits of no genuine personal relationships, only more or less disguised master-slave relationships.

The connection with the ethics of the New Age becomes

clear when you compare Nietzsche's master and slave moralities with the New Age concepts of victor- and victim-consciousness.

(c) The will to power

Atheism destroys slave morality and the corresponding under-standings of reality and human nature. This, in turn, leads to nihilism.

But nihilism can take two very different forms. It can be passive, leading to the pessimistic resignation of Nietzsche's mentor, Schopenhauer. Alternatively, it can be active, cele-brating the death of meaning and values as the transition to a new age.

The key to this active response is 'will to power', which Nietzsche understood as the intelligible character of reality. It is the unitive force underlying the plurality of the cosmos. Thus it is closely related to *eros*, the pagan concept of unitive love.

When Nietzsche looked at the world around him, will to power was the key which unlocked its meaning. In his cosmos, there is no objective meaning or truth. So what is knowledge? Knowledge is power: the will to power is manifested in the human activity of knowing. By imposing stable patterns onto the flux of reality, it turns becoming into being. All knowledge is a reading of meaning into reality. There are no absolute objective truths, only statements which, from their particular perspective, are useful fictions. Even logic itself is only a useful fiction, valid from some perspectives but not others. Again this is recognizable as a common feature of New Age thought.

Actually, such radical relativism is problematic. Consider the statement, 'All truths are fictions, including what I have just said.' It is only possible to assert the relativity of all truth from the security of an absolute standpoint. If Nietzsche were consistent he could not assert anything.

(d) Power, morality and the superman

Nietzsche presented the death of God as an indictment. He also pronounced sentence on God's killers: consistency demands that they put themselves in God's place.

Is not the greatness of this deed [the murder of God] too great for us? Must we not ourselves become gods simply to seem worthy of it? There has never been a greater deed – and whoever shall be born after us, for the sake of this deed he shall be part of a higher history than all history hitherto.[16]

Nietzsche's nihilism is optimistic. The death of God has released the unlimited potential of humankind. The destruction of objective values and truth forces man to become the creator of his own values and truths. It points towards the emancipation of the heroic individual from the resentment, morality, and persecution of the herd.

Unfettered by custom or conscience, the truly strong man is free to pursue whatever he wills to do. Such an individual is constantly striving to overcome himself as he reaches for new heights of self-transcendence. This is Nietzsche's Superman (or, more accurately, Overman).

Nietzsche's view of man is unashamedly élitist and, one might add, sexist: he is interested in the superior man who is not afraid of self-affirmation. But what of the mediocre majority? They are recognized as a necessary foundation for true culture, just as the economy and culture of classical Greece were founded upon the institution of slavery.

In spite of the fact that many New Agers appear to be egalitarian, Nietzsche's heroic path to self-deification retains considerable appeal. It is essentially the same view of humankind as is to be found in EST and its various New Age derivatives.

The myth of the superman is also dangerously susceptible to racist corruption. Nietzsche did not regard the superman as the next step in the evolutionary process. On the contrary, he represents man's daring to stand against and so transcend mere biological evolution. This capacity, this will to power was, in his view, the birthright of a spiritual élite within every race. In fact he specifically cites the Brahmin caste amongst the Hindus as a prime example of what he means. However, under the Nazis, the myth of the superman gave life to their notorious doctrine of racial superiority.

Part III

The Churches and the New Age

Christ in the New Age

1. INTRODUCTION

Christians may be surprised to discover the high regard in which
Jesus Christ appears to be held by some New Ages. This is
by no means limited to those who call themselves New Age
Christians or Christian New Agers. A similar respect is to be
found amongst many of the individuals and groups inspired
by theosophy and anthroposophy. Furthermore, many spirit
channels regularly receive messages from the ascended Jesus.

Clearly an examination of what New Agers believe about
Jesus Christ will be essential to any treatment of the interaction
between the New Age movement and Christianity.

2. THE COSMIC CHRIST AND CHRIST CONSCIOUSNESS

The New Age movement does not possess a single uniform
understanding of the Christ. Different authors and groups present the Christ in different ways – some presentations are more
'scientific' in tone, others more mythological. For the purposes
of analysis, we may identify three main approaches. But, in
practice, these different understandings of the Christ overlap
and run into each other to a considerable extent.

(a) Christ as divine energy

Typical of this approach is the following statement from a
leading Christian New Ager:

To engage in conscious struggle for the 'uncovering and discovering' of the I AM or true Self is to become aligned with the Divine activity operating in all creation. This Divine activity is what Christians call the Christ.

This Christ principle may be defined as an energy, not an impersonal energy but the highest of all energies, that of love. This energy is seeking to manifest itself at all levels of creation through the process of evolution.[1]

The author goes on to detail the unfolding of the Christ principle in terms reminiscent of Teilhard de Chardin.

Biblical justification for this understanding of Christ as energy is sought in the Johannine concept of the *Logos*. Arguing from the Hellenistic background of this concept, it is presented as the controlling principle and source of rational order of the world. Thus, in an evolutionary cosmos, it is identified with the driving force behind novelty and self-actualization.

Such an understanding of Christ is not restricted to New Age sources. As the following quotation indicates, process theology takes a similar line:

The Logos is immanent in all things as the initial phase of their subjective aim, that is, as their fundamental impulse towards actualization. . . . But in living persons a new feature appears: The initial aim is at a relevant novelty rather than a reenactment. The novelty that is aimed at is one that allows maximum incorporation of elements from the past in a new synthesis. This novelty must struggle for actualization against habit, anxiety and defensiveness. To whatever extent the new aim is successful, to that extent there is creative transformation. This creative transformation is Christ.[2]

(b) Christ as a state of consciousness

This understanding of Christ is very clear in the literature of the 'I AM' movement. This movement consists of a number of religious groups inspired by theosophy. Gordon Melton considers it 'one of the most important forerunners of the contemporary New Age movement'.[3]

For example, the Christ Self is defined as:

> The individualized focus of 'the only begotten of the Father
> full of grace and truth' (John 1:14); the universal Christ
> individualized as the true identity of the soul; the *Real Self*
> of every man, woman, and child to which the soul must rise.
> The Christ Self is the mediator between a man and his God;
> it is a man's own personal mentor, priest and prophet, master
> and teacher. Total identification with the Christ Self defined
> the Christed one, the Christed being, or the *Christ Con-
> sciousness*.[4]

The definition comes from a channelled source, Kuthumi
(apparently the same being who inspired Alice Bailey). However, it reads like a crude version of Jung's archetype of the
Self. It certainly functions in a similar way as the true centre
of the psyche through which all our knowledge of God is
mediated.

This view of Christ is complementary with the previous
understanding. The Christ consciousness is the individual manifestation of the universal Christ within each psyche. But behind
it lies the universal Christ which, according to Mark and Eliza-
beth Clare Prophet, is 'the universal consciousness of God that
went forth as the Word, the Logos that God used to fire the
pattern of His Divine Identity in His sons and daughters and
to write His laws in their inward parts'.[5] This is very similar to
the popular misconception of Jung's collective unconscious as a
mystical substratum for individual consciousnesses. Ultimately
there is one Christ: the God consciousness. But that one Christ
is individualized in the many Christ Selfs. One ocean, many
waves. This is eastern monism mated with half-understood analytical psychology and expressed in Christian language.

(c) Christ as a mythical being

Some New Agers speak of Christ as a being. For example, Sir
George Trevelyan presents the Christ in the following terms
(borrowed and simplified from Rudolf Steiner, the founder of
anthroposophy):

Who and what is the Christos? Clearly an exalted being of Light and Truth must overlight *all* mankind. He must illumine every race, creed and nation. . . .

The name 'the Christos' is Greek for this Exalted Being of the Spiritual Sun. The worship of the Spirit of Light and Truth is common to all the great religions, . . .

. . . behind all manifestation in the diversity of the relative-world is the great Oneness of Creative Intelligence and Spirit, the Divine Source. . . .

Thus the celestial bodies are not mere gaseous balls but are the spheres of action of exalted spiritual beings. . . .

The field of action of the highest hierarchy, the Elohim, is the Sun. . . . The Lord of these sublime beings is He who is known as the Christos, the Son of God.[6]

So the Christ is the Lord of a hierarchy of spiritual beings. But Trevelyan, following Steiner, envisages God as Almighty Mind. All of reality emanates from the divine consciousness as the expression of the divine ideas. The first and highest of those emanations is the Christ, the Lord of the nine heavenly hierarchies of angels. Thus, this being might better be described as the primordial expression of the divine Mind.

Trevelyan cites Pseudo-Dionysius in addition to Steiner as his authority for this elaborate scheme of emanations. However, he might equally have cited one of the Gnostic teachers of the early centuries AD (e.g., Irenaeus ascribes a very similar system to Basilides).

The main difference between this New Age approach to the Christ and Gnosticism is the former's rejection of dualism. In traditional Gnosticism matter is evil, created in ignorance by one of the lesser spirits and acting as a prison for other spiritual beings. Trevelyan takes a more positive view of matter: it is part of the divine plan, the material universe is more of a school-room for spirits than a prison.

Trevelyan and other New Agers do not hide their debt to the Gnostics. On the contrary, they cite the Gnostics as brave souls who kept alive the true teachings of Jesus in the face of mounting persecution from an increasingly institutional and unspiritual Church. Their indebtedness is reflected in the fact that the best selling title from one major publisher of New Age literature is a translation of the Nag Hammadi Gospels (a set of Gnostic scriptures).

3. JESUS, THE ENLIGHTENED MASTER

What relationship does the Christ bear to Jesus, the carpenter's son from Nazareth?

Some New Agers, including Trevelyan, see Jesus as an immensely important historical figure. His ministry represents a turning point in the spiritual history of the world because, in him, the cosmic Christ found the perfect human instrument for his redemptive activity.

Jesus was carefully prepared for this role by the Holy Spirit. Trevelyan takes the Gospel birth narratives to imply that Jesus was the end product of a long process of divinely guided selective breeding. Furthermore, the human Jesus had to be trained to play his part by initiation into the appropriate occult mysteries. Since the Gospels say nothing about the adolescence and young adulthood of Jesus, New Agers and their theosophical predecessors have driven the most amazing diversity of speculation into this period. What did he do with those missing years? Where did he spend them?

An early explanation favoured by nineteenth-century theosophists, and still the most credible of the speculations on offer, is that he spent those years with the Essenes. Trevelyan partially adheres to this explanation. He assures us (on the strength of evidence from the spirit channel, Edgar Cayce) that 'Mary was taken into the protection of the [Essene] Brotherhood and that Jesus was accepted as their highest initiate, not needing to go through their full training because he knew it all'.[7] His account of Essene teaching and practice is remarkable only in its complete disregard of historical evidence.

But where did Jesus pick up his knowledge if he already 'knew it all' at the time of his Essene initiation? The most popular explanation today is that, like so many New Agers, he went east. He studied yoga with a Hindu guru; he visited Tibet and was recruited into the Great White Brotherhood; or he was initiated into the 6000 year old Sarmoung Brotherhood of Armenia (the mythical source of Sufi wisdom). Trevelyan suggests that he was initiated into Kahuna wisdom (the native magic of Polynesia, now only preserved in Hawaii).

The crucial point in the relationship between Jesus and the Christ is held to be the baptism by John. Having been bred and trained for the role, he was now ready for the Christ to enter and take possession. Trevelyan says of the baptism:

> Then the individuality of Jesus gave place to the Christ Being, the Cosmic 'I AM'. At the moment when 'the Holy Ghost descended in the form of a dove' this Exalted Being took over the human body. For the next three years it is the Christ who is speaking in Jesus. The previous thirty years had been a preparation of the vessel.[8]

However, the possession of the physical body of Jesus by the Christ is not the whole story. New Agers who stand in the theosophical tradition bring with them a complicated understanding of the human body as consisting of several different bodies existing on different planes of reality but, as it were, superimposed. Various moments in the ministry of Jesus are explained as stages in the gradual possession of these more subtle bodies by the Christ, culminating in the triumphant cry on the Cross: the point at which matter was fully mastered, the incarnation fully achieved, and death conquered.

4. THE PLACE OF THE CROSS IN AQUARIAN THOUGHT

But what place can the Cross have in such a world-view? The Gnostic theologian, Basilides, clearly thought that it had no place. In his theology, Christ changed places with Simon of Cyrene on the way to Golgotha. Simon was mistakenly crucified in Jesus' place because the crowds were under an illusion that he was Jesus. And Jesus, now in the visible form of Simon, stood and laughed at the scene.

Steiner and many New Agers after him do, however, manage to find a role for the Cross. But, like Teilhard, they put the emphasis mainly on the incarnation itself. The incarnation is called a redemptive act, but by that they mean something other than the Christian concept of redemption. Christians believe that Christ redeemed us from our bondage to sin. For Trevelyan redemption is a metaphysical activity – it does not release us from bondage to sin; it does not conquer evil; no, it redeems us from matter.

As part of his spiritual evolution, man has chosen to descend into matter and become incarnate on earth. However, left to ourselves we would not be able to break free of its gravity. The incarnation of the Christ is a redemptive act in the sense that it introduces a counter to the gravity that hinders our spiritual evolution. Thus, the incarnation makes it possible for us to exert the effort necessary to ascend back to the spiritual realms.

Rudolf Steiner attempted to explain the incarnation in homoeopathic terms (that 'like cures like'): Christ had to become like us in order that we might become like him. That sounds like one of the theological slogans of the early Church. However, Steiner stretched the homoeopathic analogy to explain the Cross as the 'potentization' of the blood of Jesus (this is the process of dilution and shaking by which a homoeopath prepares his or her remedies). In the crucifixion, the divine blood was transmuted to an etheric level on which it could penetrate and transform the aura of the earth.

Given the strong spiritualizing tendency of New Age thought one would expect the resurrection to come in for reinterpretation – and indeed it does. It no longer holds out the promise of a future general physical resurrection. Rather it was the miraculous animation of a corpse intended to demonstrate the power of spirit over matter. 'By so doing He demonstrated that man will in time be able to overcome death and de-materialize the physical sheath when it has done its task'.[9]

This account of Jesus Christ's redemptive activity implies that evil is to be understood as imprisonment in matter. The New Agers who promote this view admit the existence of Satanic impulses, but these are bent on binding us ever more closely to matter so that our evolution is retarded. Some postulate a duality of Satanic forces, personalized as Ahriman and Lucifer. The former is the denier of spirit, the force of negation.

The latter is the personification of lust for power. However, the Christ does not destroy these evil impulses but rather tames them. They are natural impulses and essential to life – their destructiveness is merely a function of their being uncontrolled. To complicate the matter further, some New Agers identify Lucifer with the Christ impulse and speak of the transition to the New Age as a mass Luciferic initiation.

This concept of salvation is gnostic in that it assumes that what we lack is knowledge of the true state of affairs effected by the incarnation. It is also Pelagian since it claims that, given the appropriate knowledge, we are completely equipped to overcome matter for ourselves. It is up to us – we must make the effort.

5. THE FUNCTION OF NEW AGE CHRISTOLOGY

The Norwegian theologian Arild Romarheim suggests that New Age speculations about Jesus Christ serve a dual purpose: 'The Aquarian portrait of "Jesus the Christ" serves as a double legitimation for new religious movements. On the one hand, it justifies opposition against the established Church. On the other, it confirms the necessity and the plausibility of their own new spiritual movement.'[10]

(a) Casting doubt upon Christianity

Some groups associated with this view of Christ do take an aggressive stance in relation to orthodox Christianity. For example, the Church Universal and Triumphant (the most prominent of the 'I AM' groups) argues that the doctrine of substitutionary atonement is a remnant of paganism.

More common is the accusation that Christianity has radically falsified the teaching of Jesus. For example, it is often suggested that Jesus taught reincarnation but that this was suppressed by the Second Council of Constantinople in 553 AD. In fact, it was not reincarnation but belief in the existence of souls prior to conception which was condemned.

The Church is also accused of wrongly casting Jesus in the

role of a God whereas, in New Age terms, he was merely one (and not necessarily the greatest) of a brotherhood of enlightened teachers. In Blavatsky's account of the Great White Brotherhood, Master Jesus is one of the Lesser Masters subordinate to Maha Chohan (who is responsible for mediating divine intelligence to earth). However, it appears that these are titles rather than personal names for more recent accounts promote Jesus of Nazareth to the post of Bodhisattva Maitreya – his former position of Master Jesus being taken by the classical pagan sorcerer Apollonius of Tyana.

(b) Confirming New Age belief

Romarheim also suggests that the Aquarian Christ confirms the plausibility of New Age beliefs and organizations.

We are living at a time when sectarianism and cultural fragmentation have led to the loss of any public plausibility structure or world-view. A similar situation obtained in the early centuries AD and, with it, a similar proliferation of religious movements.

For some New Agers this reinterpretation of Jesus creates a plausible role model: Jesus becomes the perfect example of what all may achieve by engaging in New Age psychotechnologies. By rewriting the Christian tradition they create for themselves an authoritative myth which reinforces their world-view.

I believe that closely related to this positive role there is a third function which Romarheim has not touched on. By invoking the name of Jesus they are tapping a potent source of authority (at least for anyone brought up in a Christian country). The name acts as a bridge point – an apologetic and 'evangelistic' device. It allows the New Ager to say to the Christian, 'We are talking about the same reality. We have direct spiritual contact with the one to whom you pay lip-service. The New Age is not the contradiction of Christianity but the rediscovery of its inner core.' Significantly, the New Age Christ is completely interchangeable with any messianic figure in any other world religion.

6. NEW AGE ADOPTIONISM

The New Age understanding of Jesus Christ is not new at all. On the contrary, it is one of the oldest Christological heresies, namely, adoptionism. This is the belief that Jesus of Nazareth was a man who was adopted as son by God. In its New Age form, God deemed him fit to become the vessel for the incarnation of the cosmic Christ by virtue of his perfect grasp of the occult mysteries.

Adoptionism was rejected by the early Church because it soon became apparent that it undermined the whole spectrum of Christian belief.

That it blurs the distinction between Christ and spirit is clear from the fact that incarnation becomes indistinguishable from inspiration and demon-possession. In fact, it was often held in conjunction with an explicit or implicit unitarian theology.

It also blurs the orthodox distinction between the natural sonship of Jesus and the adoptive relationship of believers. While this may be acceptable to New Agers who want to stress their own divinity, it undermines traditional Christian understandings of redemption.

Transforming Christianity:
New Age in the Churches

1. INTRODUCTION

In spite of their affinities with eastern mysticism and occultism, New Age ideas and practices have made significant inroads into Christianity. An increasing number of Christians are prepared to call themselves New Age Christians or Christian New Agers. Many more have been influenced consciously or unconsciously by aspects of the New Age.

(a) The motives of New Age Christians

Why have so many churchgoers been attracted to a phenomenon which, in some respects at least, is clearly at variance with orthodox Christian theology?

A significant part of the answer is that, for many of these people, the New Age phenomenon is evidence of renewed spiritual interest outside the structures of institutional religion. They welcome it as an activity of the Holy Spirit and even regard it as the counterpart of the renewal movement within the churches.[1] For many of them it seems to promise a way out of the cul-de-sac in which they perceive western Christianity to be trapped.

The New Age appears to be liberal in the best sense of the word: it is generous, open, accepting of outsiders, affirming and inclusive. Men and women who feel marginalized by Christian orthodoxy but who still long for a spiritual dimension to their lives are made to feel welcome by the New Age. It appears more liberal than Christian orthodoxy and more spiritual than Christian liberalism.

Many Christian New Agers also see their involvement in the New Age as an evangelistic opportunity. Here is an undirected popular spiritual movement: Christianity has something to offer these people. They would agree with the sentiments of Bishop Stephen Verney: 'The "New Age" thinking can be of God, or it can be demonic.' Christ must become 'the "Saviour" of the "New Age" movement as of everything else. Without him we tend to go the way of Lucifer'.[2] They hope that by allying themselves with the New Age they can give the phenomenon direction and at the same time revitalize the Christian faith.

A third factor which is often overlooked by critics of New Age Christianity is the internal diversity of the Christian religion. Many New Age Christians are not so much looking outside their tradition for spiritual nourishment as reappropriating neglected aspects of Christianity. Their spiritual inspiration comes not from the *Upanishads* or the *Tao te Ching* but from the Christian mystics: men and women such as Hildegard of Bingen, Julian of Norwich, Meister Eckhardt, and Jacob Boehme. In effect their experience of the New Age has been one of liberation to look at their own tradition with fresh eyes.

(b) Responding to New Age Christianity

Unfortunately the overwhelming orthodox response to such explorations has been one of recrimination and accusation. New Age Christians are commonly accused of 'selling out', of betraying the faith and leading others into error.

This accusation has become a convenient stick with which to beat Christians whose views differ from our own. Some Christians seem to see the phrase 'New Age' not as a description but as a judgement. By using the label in this way they rule out any possibility of genuine debate.

Christian charity and justice demand that we treat such accusations with caution. If a particular individual or group is labelled in this way we should take pains to find out just what they do believe. Sympathetic understanding is the only legitimate basis for criticism.

2. LETTING A HUNDRED FLOWERS GROW

St James's Church, Piccadilly, is frequently cited as a prime British example of New Age Christianity. Tony Higton concludes his account of St James's in the following terms:

It is fertile soil for the growth of New Age ideas and influence. The fact that this is allowed in an Anglican church is, of course, a scandal of the first order. But the spineless 'tolerance' of much Anglicanism not only leaves the door open to New Age infiltration; it puts out the welcome mat.[3]

The basis for these accusations is the Alternatives programme which holds regular meetings at St James's. This is a New Age network whose organisers have close associations with Findhorn.[4] Its programme of lectures, workshops, and meditations is a microcosm of the New Age phenomenon in the UK, with speakers such as Sir George Trevelyan, David Spangler, Caitlin Matthews, Rupert Sheldrake, and Starhawk.

However the relationship between Alternatives and St James's is not as straightforward as Higton and others make out. The programme of Alternatives displays a prominent disclaimer: 'Although St James's Church, in its generosity and openness of mind, hosts Alternatives, the ideas in the Alternatives programme are not representative of St James's Church itself.' In a response to an attack published in the magazine *Prophecy Today*, the rector of St James's, Donald Reeves, described the relationship between the church and Alternatives as one of hospitality.

Reeves clearly sees that ministry as potentially evangelistic for he comments:

I know of many who have found Christ through the hospitality we have offered. It is a difficult ministry, easily misunderstood and sometimes, as I have often said and freely admit, we have made mistakes. We are the only church in the United Kingdom which provides this sort of hospitality for the New Age.[5]

On my visits to Alternatives at St James's I have been struck by the fact that Reeves who is usually conspicuously present at

Christian meetings in the church has been conspicuously absent. Unfortunately also apparently absent is the element of confrontation which is necessary if such hospitality is to be genuinely evangelistic.

Tony Higton questions Reeves' assertion that many have found Christ in this way, insinuating that the Christ they have encountered is some New Age counterfeit.[6] Such allegations are hard to substantiate. What is clear, however, is that if people have become Christians through this ministry it is in spite of rather than because of Alternatives. Their way seems to be that of Mao Tse-Tung: 'Letting a hundred flowers grow and a hundred schools of thought contend is the policy'.

3. THE OMEGA ORDER: CHRISTIANITY FOR A NEW AGE?

The Omega Order was founded in 1980 by Canon Peter Spink, a former missionary in India, Canon of Coventry Cathedral, and Warden of the Burrswood Home of Healing. In its introductory literature it describes itself as a contemplative and teaching order standing 'within the tradition of western Catholic Christianity'. This suggests that in some sense it adheres to the creeds promulgated by the ecumenical councils of the Christian Church.

More specifically Peter Spink claims that the Order takes inspiration from the writings of F. C. Happold and Teilhard de Chardin: 'Happold's proposition that a leap epoch is now taking place in human evolution resulting in a profound change of consciousness, and Teilhard's perception of a new Christ-consciousness, combine to give the Order its vision'.[7]

Again its introductory literature claims that 'through the discipline of contemplative awareness it seeks to touch the essence of the Catholic faith and to relate this to the new Christ consciousness now operating beyond the ecclesiastical boundaries.' In other words it exists to build bridges between orthodox Christianity and the New Age. This purpose is further underlined by the operating guidelines of the Order which include recognizing Christ 'under all forms to the exclusion of none' and encouraging 'the Christ consciousness wherever it may be found'.

The recurring references to Christ consciousness rather than to the historical Jesus Christ inevitably ring warning bells in the minds of orthodox Christians. What is meant by Christ consciousness and how does it relate to Jesus Christ? Answers to these questions become apparent as we begin to examine Peter Spink's published writings.

It appears that Christ consciousness is an attitude of mind: 'the attitude of mind which refuses to allow the least concession to, or belief in evil'.[8] It is the alignment of the personality with the Christ principle which he defines as divine energy (or love) immanent in creation.[9]

Jesus of Nazareth operated consistently on this level of consciousness throughout his life. In him we see 'a complete aligning of the human individuality or ego with this Divine Principle'.[10] Thus we may speak of Jesus as incarnating the Christ principle.

It is possible that he is attempting to express orthodox Christian belief in language accessible to New Agers. If so he has failed to indicate the points at which the Christian view of Jesus differs from that of the New Age. Teilhard is cited as one of the inspirations of the Order, but he was always very clear on the uniqueness of the incarnation. Such clarity is absent from Spink's writings.

Another question mark about the Order relates to the source of its inspiration. Happold and Teilhard are singled out in the introductory literature but do not figure prominently in Spink's writings. The thinkers who do take centre stage include Alice Bailey, Rudolf Steiner, Gurdjieff, and several of Gurdjieff's disciples (including Ouspensky, Assagioli, J. G. Bennett, and Kathleen Speeth). It appears that his interpretation of Christianity relies heavily upon some of the most important forerunners of the New Age. Indeed at one point he asserts that 'no theological studies which operate without reference to the anthroposophical insights which modern man owes chiefly to such seers as Rudolf Steiner, and bodies such as the Theosophical Society, can properly comprehend the origin, source and significance of the new understanding . . .'[11]

The affinity with theosophy is also apparent in the Omega Invocation:

> May the Light that shows the way
> illuminate the mind.
>
> May the Love that knows the truth
> unfold within the heart.
>
> May the Power that gives true life
> arise within the soul.
>
> Let Light and Love and Power
> raise all in Christ to God.

This is described as a prayer based on John 14:6 and it is true that way, truth and life have been inserted into the structure. But the structure itself owes more to New Age invocations such as the Great Invocation and the Glastonbury Invocation.[12] Specifically, the triad of Light, Love and Power which shapes this invocation is a recurring feature of New Age invocations.

5. CREATION-CENTRED SPIRITUALITY

By virtue of its international influence, this is probably the most important bridge point between Christianity and the New Age. Creation-centred spirituality[13] is a popular movement inspired by an American Dominican priest, Matthew Fox.

Fox's interest in developing a creation-affirming spirituality dates back to his doctoral studies in Paris where he sat at the feet of M. D. Chenu, a distinguished Roman Catholic church historian. It took on a feminist/liberation theology dimension as a result of teaching in an American women's college.

In 1977 he founded the Institute in Culture and Creation Spirituality. The staff of that Institute gives some idea of Fox's eclecticism: in addition to Starhawk it boasts a Voudun priestess, a Native American medicine man, and a Zen Buddhist. A similar eclecticism may be seen in its British counterpart, the Centre for Creation Spirituality at St James's Church, Piccadilly: it recently sponsored a festival of pagan Celtic spirituality which included an introduction to Druid magic, a display of paintings depicting Celtic aspects of the Goddess, and lectures by the New Age witch, Caitlin Matthews.

The emphasis of creation spirituality is largely practical and experiential rather than theological. Thus it is easily accessible to the average layman. It achieved a certain notoriety in 1984, when Fox came to the attention of the Sacred Congregation for the Doctrine of the Faith (formerly the Holy Office of the Inquisition). At present he remains under investigation.

(a) The four paths

Fox invites us to embark upon a pilgrimage along four spiritual paths which he describes as befriending creation; befriending darkness; befriending creativity; and befriending new creation.[14]

He claims that these paths represent the spiritual tradition of Jesus himself: a tradition which has consistently been suppressed by the institutional church. Reclaiming this tradition for contemporary Christianity will, he promises, open up new possibilities for the solution not only of deep rifts within the Christian faith but also for global problems of social justice and ecology.

(i) *Befriending creation* is presented as a counter-balance to what he perceives as the Church's dualistic hatred of the material world and its corollary, asceticism. He calls on us to see creation as a blessing rather than a curse. It is God's gift to us, to be enjoyed; not a prison which separates the soul from God.

(ii) *Befriending darkness* is very similar to the *via negativa* of traditional Christian spirituality. It involves the giving up of our images and words to find God in silence and the luminous darkness of Christian mysticism.

But it also involves the acceptance of pain. By working through our pain instead of suppressing it we become more sensitive to the pain of others, both human and nonhuman. Pain burns away false pleasures; enables us to endure; creates bonds of compassion. For Fox, this is the way of the Cross.

(iii) *Befriending creativity* moves us on to a more active

spirituality. Like so many Christians today, Fox identifies our creativity with the divine image in us. Thus he also calls this path, 'befriending our divinity'. He recommends artistic activity as a form of meditation. Nor is it limited to what is conventionally understood as art; our whole lives are to be seen as works of art beautifying God's good creation.

(iv) *Befriending new creation* is the fourth and last stage of Fox's plan. Like the previous stage it is active. It calls upon us to look outwards to the world. It calls upon us to work out our Christian faith in the very practical activity of seeking personal, social, and ecological justice.

(b) The underlying theology

On the face of it, Fox offers us an attractive spirituality. He rightly turns away from the tendency to despise the body which has been prevalent in western spirituality. Similarly his insistence on linking spirituality with the way we live and relate to others is a valuable corrective to the tendency to view spirituality as something private, entirely between the individual and God. However, as we shall see, all that glitters is not gold.

Fox clearly identifies creation with nature and this entails a radical revision of our understanding of God. The route taken by Fox is to espouse panentheism (the belief that all things are in God). He is motivated by a desire to root out dualism which he sees in the classical theistic contrast between Creator and creation.

In using this concept he hopes to avoid the heresy of pantheism. However, the symbolism he adopts for speaking about God is overwhelmingly horizontal. Panentheism claims to maintain God's transcendence along with a greater stress on his immanence. But Fox's manner of speaking about God fails to do justice to that transcendence. The impression is that God is to be sought within (within the world, within the human unconscious) rather than through the world. There is little or no sense that God is beyond the world.

The radical immanence of God is also implicit in Fox's understanding of *dabhar*, divine creative energy, or 'original blessing'. This energy infuses all of creation. It flows through everything, uniting creatures with one another and with their divine ground. Fox variously describes this energy as the power of fertility and the desire behind creation. He even goes so far as to identify it with *eros* (the cosmic force which, in Hellenistic thought, causes the multiplicity of creation to strive after divine unity). Thus this aspect of his thought has affinities with Nietzsche's 'will to power'. As one would expect, Fox adheres to the principle of interconnectedness and even celebrates its monistic tendencies.

Just how important this concept is to Fox is clear from the way he allows it to transform his understanding of the relationship between God and creation (particularly human creatures). Since divine energy flows through all things and is the reality of which words are merely symbolic, 'We are part of that flow and we need to listen to it rather than to assume arrogantly that our puny words are the only words of God'.[15] By 'our puny words' he means the Judaeo-Christian Scriptures (and, indeed, the scriptures of every other religion). Since God's energy is prior to mere words, creation must take priority over revelation as the source of our theology and spirituality.

A corollary of this is that the path to God begins with ecstatic immersion in creation. In this way, 'We become like the Creator and take on the Creator's characteristics'.[16] This suggests that Fox's revision of Christian theology must extend to his concept of salvation.

Salvation, for Fox, is emphatically not a process of being redeemed from a fallen state. He rejects the whole edifice of fall/redemption spirituality and theology as fundamental to the dualism he seeks to overcome. Indeed, for Fox, a fall/redemption mentality is the very root of sin, leading, in his view, to 'sexism, militarism, racism, genocide against native peoples, biocide, consumerist capitalism, and violent communism'.[17]

On the contrary we need to be saved from our enslavement to the notion of fall and redemption. This salvation is achieved by the awakening of *eros*. As our desire for unity is brought to life by the exploration of sexuality, the arts, dance, *T'ai Chi*, yoga, shamanistic rituals, or any of the myriad consciousness altering techniques currently available we begin to experience our oneness. We overcome all the pernicious dualities of western thought. The distinctions between body and soul, man and woman, human and nonhuman, creature and God are dissolved.

Fox's rhetoric is clearly designed to appeal to those who are in sympathy with New Age thinking rather than traditional Christianity. Speaking of the contemporary explosion of New Consciousness, he comments that, 'If entire religious bodies such as Christianity could enter into this expanding spiritual energy field, there is no predicting what powers of passion and compassion might become unleashed'.[18]

At the same time he launches a vitriolic attack on Augustine's influence on western Christianity. He presents a gross oversimplification and distortion of the relationship between fall/redemption spirituality and creation spirituality within western Christianity. The very theologians he celebrates as representatives of the minority creation tradition (e.g., Hildegard of Bingen) were also staunch advocates of fall/redemption spirituality. A more accurate view would be that the two have co-existed in tension with one another. It is when one or other of the two traditions has been suppressed that the Church has lurched towards heresy. One is left with the uneasy feeling that this is not so much Christian spirituality as New Age thought in Christian trappings.

Building Up the Dividing Walls
of Hostility: The Way of Reaction

1. HOSTILITY TO THE NEW AGE

While some Christians have welcomed the New Age movement, a more common response has been rejection. This is
often expressed in highly emotive terms: a 'coming age of
barbarism', 'darkness', some critics have even attempted to
associate New Agers with human sacrifice! Typical is the following summary comment from Randall Baer (a former New
Ager):

> Essentially, it is a satan-controlled, modern-day mass revival
> of occult based philosophies and practices in both obvious
> and cleverly disguised forms. In effect, it is an end-times
> 'plague of the spirit' . . . NA philosophy and practices have
> crept into the very fabric of society in both subtle and pro-
> found ways. The magnitude and momentum of this move-
> ment is to such an extent that it poses one of the fastest
> growing threats to Christianity today.[1]

The popularity of such views is clear from the proliferation
of conspiracy theories, accusing New Agers of plotting the take-
over of the world. Another indicator is the level of sales
enjoyed by Frank Peretti's occult conspiracy novels, *This Present Darkness* and *Piercing the Darkness*.

This is by no means exclusively a fundamentalist response to
the New Age. Covert hostility to the New Age transcends all
theological barriers. One senior Anglican churchman recently
dismissed the New Age as 'religious junk food'. Such a refusal

to take people's spiritual aspirations seriously is no less hostile than accusing them of being involved in a satanic conspiracy.

Ironically, hostility to the New Age is also found amongst members of the occult establishment. They too are likely to dismiss New Age claims about spiritual experiences or even view it as a threat to genuine occult philosophy. Typical would be the following comment: ' "new agers" might be defined as rather amateur gnostics . . . In general "old fashioned" occultists like myself tend to take the New Age with a pinch of salt. Too much of it is hype, and not very well thought out hype at that'.[2]

2. CONSPIRACY THEORIES

My dictionary defines 'conspiracy' as:

> 1. The action of conspiring. 2. . . . . A combination of persons for an evil or unlawful purpose; an agreement between two or more to do something criminal, illegal, or reprehensible; a plot; a body of conspirators

Marilyn Ferguson is usually credited with applying this epithet to the New Age movement. However, she portrays it as a leaderless coalition of networks and pressure groups whose members are united by shared spiritual experiences. Clearly her use of the term 'conspiracy' was intended as nothing more than a piece of journalistic sensationalism.

However, Ferguson's terminology was taken seriously by Christians alarmed at the rapid growth of the New Age movement. A former attorney, Constance Cumbey, responded by writing *Hidden Dangers of the Rainbow*, a book which has become a seminal contribution to the New Age conspiracy genre. Contrary to Ferguson, she argues that 'the abundance of network council organizational charts, matrixes, statements of purpose, and directories' are indicative of 'leadership and structure to an advanced degree'.[3] Cumbey summarizes her accusation against the New Age thus:

> It is the contention of this writer that for the first time . . .

there is a viable movement – the New Age Movement – that truly meets the scriptural requirements for the antichrist and the political movement that will bring him on the world scene. . . . It is further contended . . . that this Movement has infiltrated all of Christianity.[4]

(a) A political conspiracy?

Cumbey claims that the New Age movement is a political conspiracy in the conventional sense of the word. Its apparent diversity is dismissed as a deliberate smoke-screen covering a neo-Nazi political programme.[5] She argues that a single organization directs the entire New Age and implies that *Planetary Citizens* is that group.[6]

Cumbey cites as evidence the existence of various open admissions that such a conspiracy exists. Ferguson's book is presented as an important recent example. But, this aspect of her case rests upon the writings of Alice Bailey and a late work of H. G. Wells (*The Open Conspiracy*). Wells' book sketches one way in which global government might be achieved. More important is Bailey's insistence on the existence of a 'Plan' to bring about a world religion as well as a world government. Cumbey claims that the New Age movement follows Bailey's 'Plan' 'like a recipe'.[7]

Also important to Cumbey's case is the New Age practice of networking and the many New Age directories. She interprets these directories as evidence that the movements and organizations cited are all part of the conspiracy.

What about the evidence for New Age infiltration into the churches? Cumbey is not content to restrict her accusations to controversial figures like Matthew Fox. Taking Ferguson as her authority, she claims that covert New Agers recognize and communicate with one another by means of code words (e.g., holistic, transformation, Spaceship Earth, Global Village, interdependence, manifestation, initiation, crowded planet, transcendent, consciousness-raising, (new) paradigm, (planetary, global, new) vision, and transpersonal[8]). By seeking out such terms in Christian literature she has identified several leading evangelicals (e.g., Ron Sider) as covert New Agers.

She also accuses World Vision and Inter-Varsity Christian Fellowship of having a New Age orientation.[9]

Cumbey employs her legal skills to weave a case against the New Age. However, the adversarial tactics of the courtroom are ill-suited to determining the truth or otherwise of such accusations. Serious questions must be asked about the value of her 'evidence'.

To begin with, the very openness of the 'conspirators' raises doubts about her evidence for a conspiracy. What sort of conspiracy allows its key members to divulge large portions of its plan in best-selling books? Furthermore, given that many New Agers seem keen to publicize their 'conspiracy', Cumbey's reliance on their testimony seems naive. Is their testimony reliable?

The range of interpretations currently on offer raises doubts about the reliability of the evidence. Both extremes of the political spectrum have been implicated in the conspiracy: Cumbey holds neo-Nazi influences responsible, while others see the New Age as a Communist plot. A similarly broad spectrum of religious organizations is implicated, ranging from theosophy to Roman Catholicism.[10] If the available literature can generate such a wide range of interpretations, it is hardly the blueprint for world domination suggested by Cumbey.

At the heart of Cumbey's case is Alice Bailey's 'Plan'. But her presentation of it as a blueprint for political action is misleading. Bailey's 'Plan' was envisaged as a spiritual rather than a political plan. Its goals were to be achieved by meditation rather than by political action (hence the importance of the Great Invocation amongst Bailey's disciples). The real conspirators are not incarnate human beings but discarnate spiritual entities (the spiritual Masters who belong to the Hierarchy or White Brotherhood). Far from encouraging temporal conspiracies such an approach effectively de-politicizes its adherents.

In her efforts to implicate evangelical leaders in this New Age conspiracy Cumbey resorts to misrepresentation. Perhaps the most outrageous example is her insinuation that Loren Wilkinson, an evangelical scholar who has written extensively on environmental matters, calls for a 'New World religion'.

The basis for her claim is a long quotation from his book *Earthkeeping* which speaks of eastern theology as a counterbalance to aspects of western Christianity. Cumbey edits the quotation to give the impression that Wilkinson is advocating 'Hindu occultism' when, in fact, he is referring to Eastern Orthodox Christianity.[11]

(b) A satanic conspiracy?

The weakness of the evidence has led many Christians to discount the political aspect of Cumbey's thesis in favour of the spiritual aspect. Her continuing reputation rests on her attempt to show that the New Age fits the parameters of biblical apocalyptic literature: she identifies it (and Nazism) with the great beast of Revelation 13.[12]

This approach has the advantage that it concurs with the testimony of a number of leading figures within the New Age movement. They see the New Age as an incredibly diverse phenomenon, a loose coalition of different pressure groups, spiritual movements and alternative therapies with no co-ordinated human leadership. However, underlying the human diversity they discern a concerted effort at the spiritual level: 'The Divine will, the energy of creation itself, is steering us in a new direction, towards the discovery of Itself within'.[13] Similar sentiments may be found in the writings of David Spangler and Sir George Trevelyan.

Many conservative Christians agree with this belief that there is an underlying spiritual will driving the entire New Age phenomenon. However, they disagree over the interpretation: it is not God but Satan who is responsible. Michael Cole typifies this view: 'Although the New Age does not have all the usual manifestations of a movement – no central organisation, no headquarters, no hierarchy, no creed – yet it is *an unholy alliance* throughout the world challenging the rule and authority of God'.[14]

By stressing that it is a spiritual conspiracy, this approach dispenses with the need for secular evidence. Indeed some writers actively discourage the search for such evidence on the grounds that it merely plays into Satan's hands.[15] Instead they turn to biblical evidence against the New Age. In the past decade a considerable amount has been written about the New Age in relation to biblical eschatology and apocalyptic.

What is often overlooked in the rush to identify the New Age with biblical symbols is that this approach assumes a particular minority interpretation of biblical apocalyptic, namely, *premillenialism*. This is perhaps the most literal way of interpreting the relevant texts and has been popularized in recent years by Hal Lindsey. It envisages a time of apostasy leading to a period of global tribulation. Then Christ will return, destroy the beast and the false prophet, and set up an earthly kingdom over which he will reign for 1000 years until the last judgement. Those who attempt to link the New Age with this eschatology see the New Age as Satan's instrument for persecuting the Church.

However, there are alternative ways of interpreting the Book of Revelation. The founders of modern evangelicalism (e.g., John Owen, Samuel Rutherford, the Wesleys, Philip Spener, and Jonathan Edwards) favoured *postmillenialism*. In this view the dawning of the Age of the Spirit precedes the End. Instead of the Church being persecuted prior to the supernatural imposition of Christ's reign, it would be the instrument of extending Christ's reign over all the earth. From a postmillenial perspective the New Age may be no more than a temporary aberration, a slight historical detour, in the steady progress towards global Christianity. Alternatively, the redemption of the New Age could be the very thing that ushers in Christ's millenial reign. In either case, far from being an object of fear and suspicion, the New Age becomes an evangelistic opportunity.

A third interpretation (favoured by Augustine and the Reformers) is *amillenialism*. According to amillenialists, the Church is the manifestation of Christ's millenial reign. While this interpretation allows for a time of persecution and tribulation immediately prior to the last judgement, it does not seek to identify the symbols of the Book of Revelation with specific movements such as the New Age. On the contrary, the Great Beast symbolizes all false religion and all purely human ideology.[16] From an amillenialist perspective, the New Age is no more and no less satanic than any other human religion or ideology.

What, then, are we to make of satanic conspiracy theories? Two things are worth noting. First, this is a metaphorical use of the word conspiracy since ultimately a single guiding will (that of Satan) rather than a coalition of wills is envisaged. It is not telling us anything useful about the structure of the New Age. Recalling the dictionary definition, the word has been chosen to convey that this is something evil. It is an expression of condemnation rather than a description. Secondly, since it depends on a particular interpretation of biblical prophecy, it serves as a covert way of promoting that interpretation within the wider Christian community.

3. THE REAL EFFECT OF CONSPIRACY THEORIES

Constance Cumbey and others in that mould are, no doubt, acting with the best of intentions. Their aims are laudable. They desire to alert Christians and others to the potential dangers of the New Age. They also want to point out what they perceive to be the possible fulfillment of biblical prophecy.

However, the device of the conspiracy theory has a very bad track record. No matter what the intentions of the authors, such theories tend to create an atmosphere of fear and suspicion amongst their readers. In turn, that atmosphere may lead to a variety of unlooked-for results.

(a) Self-fulfilling prophecies

Conspiracy theories tend to be self-fulfilling prophecies. This seems to have been the case with the Aquarian conspiracy: prior to Ferguson's book there was little sense of a New Age movement as a single entity. Instead there were many overlapping (and sometimes competing) new religious movements, occult groups, and alternative therapies. Her presentation of this farrago as a united spiritual conspiracy did much to popularize a view previously restricted to a theosophically-inspired minority of New Agers.

The role of conspirator can be attractive: it romanticizes your activities. New Agers are no longer merely spiritual eccentrics, they are members of a spiritual underground, an élite dedicated to the spiritual transformation of the human race. Christian denunciations merely serve to reinforce that romantic self-image.

The dangers of inventing conspiracy theories are explored at length in Umberto Eco's terrifying masterpiece *Foucault's Pendulum*. It is the story of a group of editors in a minor Italian publishing house which specializes in publishing occult literature. Bored by the triteness of what they are forced to publish, they invent their own occult conspiracy based on the legends of the Knights Templar. But the occultists get wind of this piece of fiction, take it for reality, and the conspiracy becomes real. Towards the end of the book the hero reflects on what they have done:

> We invented a nonexistent Plan, and They not only believed it was real but convinced themselves that They had been part of it for ages, or, rather, They identified the fragments of their muddled mythology as moments of our Plan, moments joined in a logical, irrefutable web of analogy, semblance, suspicion. . . .
>
> We offered a map to people who were trying to overcome a deep, private frustration. What frustration? Belbo's last file suggested it to me: There can be no failure if there really is a Plan. Defeated you may be, but never through any fault of your own. To bow to a cosmic will is no shame.[17]

Successful conspiracy theories weave individuals and groups into a larger pattern. For men and women seeking meaning in life, the accusation that they are conspirators in something very big indeed may function like a surrogate gospel.

Would-be conspiracy theorists would do well to study *Foucault's Pendulum*! Eco highlights the skewed logic of many conspiracy theories: concepts and events are connected not causally but by analogy; if pursued far enough, this sequence of connections will close back upon itself (the logic is circular); and the plausibility depends upon the connections having been made before (preferably many times) so that a tradition of interpretation subverts critical thought. He also challenges the conspiracy theorist to examine him- or herself:

> If you feel guilty, you invent a plot, many plots. And to counter them, you have to organize your own plot. But the more you invent enemy plots, to exonerate your lack of understanding, the more you fall in love with them, and you pattern your own on their model.[18]

(b) Demonization of others

Conspiracy theories have been used to terrifying effect as a weapon of political repression. Nazi Germany, Stalinist Russia and even the United States during the McCarthy era all resorted to such tactics.

Those who present the New Age as a Satanic conspiracy are usually quick to dissociate themselves from any suggestion that individual members are conscious agents of Satan. However, the viciousness of the attack[19] must have a knock-on effect on Christian attitudes to individual New Agers. If the New Age is a satanic conspiracy, it follows that (consciously or unconsciously) its members are satanic conspirators. They are doubly damned by the language used to describe their movement. Thus such language effectively puts New Agers beyond the pale: Christians may pray for them and act against them, but dare not befriend them lest they be tainted.

The New Age as a culture is regarded by many Christians as beyond redemption. Individual New Agers may be redeemed but only after the complete repudiation of the New Age and all its works.

This pattern is clear in the novels of Frank Peretti. In over 1000 pages, only one New Ager becomes a Christian and she was already alienated from the New Age prior to her contact with Christianity. His typical New Ager is devious if not dishonest, prepared to commit murder to further the cause, and invariably demonically inspired.

(c) Dehumanization of oneself

The fear which leads to such demonizing of others has an equally corrosive effect on one's own humanity. Again the behaviour of many law-abiding German citizens (including Christians) under Nazism is a salutary reminder of the dangers of scapegoating.

The evangelical theologian James Sire, commenting on contemporary Christian attitudes to members of new religious movements, sums up this danger:

> A siege mentality is at work. Those who hold cultic ideas are seen as the enemy, the great threat to humanity, to Christians, even some seem to suggest, to God himself . . . So in response anything goes: innuendo, name-calling, back-handed remarks, assumption of the worst motives on the part of the cult believers. And thus the Christian dehumanizes the enemy and shoots him like a dog. But the Christian in this process is himself dehumanized.[20]

The example of Constance Cumbey shows how fear of the New Age has led to a lowering of standards of evidence from those required to maintain academic integrity to the adversarial level of the courtroom. But that is the least of the dangers risked by such an approach. As Sire points out, the end rapidly comes to justify the means. Fear leads to hatred, and the justification of behaviour which cannot be justified by any biblical standard (including genocide[21]). Contrast this with the perfect love which casts out fear, and which Christians are called to exhibit to all, including New Agers.

(d) The reshaping of Christianity

(i) *Reshaping mission and evangelism*: Orthodox Christian missiology maintains that part of the uniqueness of the Christian gospel lies in its translatability. When Christian missionaries encounter a new culture or language group their first task is translation: the translation of the gospel into the language and conceptual structure of the people they are working with. As time goes on it becomes a process of dialogue as this new cultural expression of the gospel is refined and begins to challenge aspects of its new context. In other words, Christianity seeks to redeem the individual *within* his or her own culture.

You can see this process at work within the New Testament itself. The first Christians presented their faith as a form of Judaism. Gradually its radical implications became clear and the gospel spread to the Samaritans and then to the Gentiles. As it spread, it shook off its original Jewish cultural context and was re-expressed in terms of the dominant Hellenistic culture. This process occurred gradually over several centuries culminating in the ecumenical creeds which have subsequently defined orthodox Christianity.

Contrast this with Islam. When Islam is introduced to a new culture, its missionaries bend their efforts to teaching the people Arabic. Islam is tightly bound to a cultural package including the Arabic language, Islamic law, and even architectural principles.

Not so with Christianity. However, in their attitude to the New Age, many Christians seem to indicate that in this case it is so: New Agers must be redeemed *from* their culture. Implicit in this hostility to the New Age is a new view of mission, a more individualistic view of mission.

At the same time, Christian hostility to the New Age threatens to spell the death of evangelism amongst New Agers. Peretti's novels are striking not only because they depict a beleaguered Church struggling against the rising tide of New Age occultism but because they portray a Church which seems singularly unwilling to befriend New Agers or engage in personal witness to them. In their list of strategies for 'overcoming' the New Age, DeParrie and Pride do list evangelism, but they interpret it as impersonal mass proclamation of the gospel. Personal witness is conspicuous by its absence from their list.[22]

(ii) *Overemphasis on spirits and spiritual power*: Part of the response to New Age spiritualism has been a re-examination of Christian teaching on angels and demons. This is no bad thing. One of the effects of secularism has been a very real reluctance on the part of Christian theologians to take these matters seriously. This is now changing and, in part, we have the New Age's fascination with spiritual powers to thank for the change.

However, there are very real dangers connected with putting more emphasis on angels. We must take care that this emphasis does not divert us from the central truths of the Christian gospel. In particular, we must ensure that giving a greater role to created spiritual forces does not in any way detract from the completeness of Christ's victory at Calvary.

A corollary of this is a tendency towards a pagan understanding of prayer. Peretti's novels again typify this tendency by making a direct correlation between sheer quantity of prayer and the capacity of angels to act on God's behalf. At times he gives the impression that prayer is as impersonal as recharging a battery. It certainly bears little relation to the Christian understanding of prayer as the expression of a personal relationship with God.

(iii) *Purity and division*: The fear and suspicion which build barriers between Christians and New Agers also colour relationships within the Church itself. Fear of infiltration has led Christians to put greater emphasis on the purity of the visible church. Unfortunately this has resulted in political and theological differences being used as the basis for accusations of New Age infiltration.

Hostility to the New Age is not divisive in the sense that it causes fragmentation of churches. But it is increasingly being used as a yardstick of orthodoxy. Thus it becomes a device for promoting a particular brand of Christianity. Like any external threat, the perceived threat posed by the New Age, can be used as a way of creating apparent unity – the unity of the fortress, the unity of the monolith. Such a unity is a false unity built upon fear, a unity which denies the God-given diversity of the Christian faith.

4. WHY IS THE NEW AGE PERCEIVED AS A THREAT?

This is perhaps an obvious question with all too obvious answers. Nonetheless it is worth asking as an exercise in Christian self-examination.

(a) A successful rival

In the New Age we are confronted with a spiritual movement which is enjoying rapid growth amongst the very kinds of people who, a generation or two ago, might have been expected to be the backbone of institutional Christianity. The New Age is a direct competitor with Christianity in the free market of contemporary religion.

Hostility is an understandable human response to such a situation but it diverts attention from self-criticism. A more productive response might have been to ask the question 'where did we go wrong?' How can we put our house in order? How can we show that Christianity has a more satisfying answer to the spiritual longings of all these people?

Instead of answering such questions the temptation is to assume that we got everything right but did not proclaim it loudly enough.

(b) Similarities to Christian renewal

Another basis for Christian hostility is the embarrassing similarity between the New Age and the Christian renewal movement. This first struck me as I watched a video of the Harmonic Convergence at Glastonbury. Apart from the absence of explicit references to the Christian gospel, what I saw there was uncannily similar to my experiences of renewal services. The same kinds of people were there (white, middle-class, young to middle-aged, casual, smiling); there appeared to be the same atmosphere of emotional warmth, openness and acceptance; even the same kinds of behaviour were reproduced (guitar-accompanied choruses, dancing in the spirit, singing in tongues).

There are certainly a number of common practices and emphases. These include the use of creative visualization (though Christians have begun to play this down since they realized that New Agers also engage in it[23]). There are striking similarities between the affirmations of prosperity consciousness and the 'name it, frame it, claim it' approach to prayer favoured by some members of the prosperity theology movement. New Age and Christian healing techniques also show certain similarities.

Thus it is not surprising that some Christians have perceived the New Age as a satanic counterfeit of Christianity (while others have accused sections of the charismatic movement of being New Age). However, it is worth bearing in mind that, for all their diversity in detail, the range of possible spiritual exercises is finite. Such similarities may be explained as simple coincidence – the use of neutral techniques by different religious groups, for different purposes.

(c) Fear of the occult

Some Christians see New Age and other occult activities as an effective counter to the Christian gospel. Not only is it perceived to harden the hearts of participants but it may be regarded as casting a pall of spiritual deadness over an entire community, undermining evangelistic efforts. It is also perceived as an effective agent of destruction within the Church. Thus divisions within the Church, physical illness, and spiritual weakness may all be ascribed to involvement with the occult. We must beware that such attitudes do not lead us to fear the occult.

I do not wish to give the impression that hostile spiritual activity is not a very real and, at times, dangerous phenomenon. The beginning of my research into the New Age 'coincided' with a dramatic sequence of unpleasant personal experiences for my family. Nothing like that has re-occurred since the establishment of a prayer support group.

However, the New Testament gives no grounds for believing that Christians need fear occult activity. On the contrary, Paul insists that since Calvary all spiritual powers are subject to Christ. It was this conviction that enabled him to affirm, in the face of a much more perilous situation than faces us today, 'we are more than conquerors through him who loved us. For I am sure that neither death, nor life, nor angels, nor principalities, nor things present, nor things to come, nor powers, nor height, nor depth, nor anything else in all creation, will be able to separate us from the love of God in Jesus Christ our Lord' (Rom. 8:37-9).

Significantly, occultists I have met are afraid of Christian prayers. One of them specifically asked me not to pray for him on the grounds that 'the prayers of a Christian are as good as a curse'!

Confrontation in Love:
The Way of Dialogue

1. THE WAY OF DIALOGUE

(a) The example of St Paul

Acts 17:16–34 offers us a model for Christian cross-cultural communication. Paul is waiting in Athens for the arrival of his fellow missionaries, Silas and Timothy. While he waits he familiarizes himself with the local culture, institutions, and religion. He also takes every opportunity to preach the gospel.

What does this have to teach us about Christian evangelism at the end of the twentieth century?

First, Paul went to the Athenians. That may seem obvious. But his behaviour was in marked contrast to what might have been expected of an ex-Pharisee. Judaism in general, and Pharisaism in particular, did not proclaim its faith to outsiders. If Gentiles wished to learn about Judaism they were welcome in the synagogue and could become God-fearers (token Jews, adopting Jewish cultural norms in place of their native Gentile cultures).

Paul and his fellow Christians had begun the long process of disentangling Christian faith from Jewish culture. They went to the Gentiles. They operated within Hellenistic culture. They used the institutions and the modes of communication normal to that culture.

Secondly, Paul took the trouble to understand them. This is implicit in the fact that he was clearly at home in their institutions such as the Areopagus. Since he came from a Hellenistic Jewish background, he would already be broadly familiar with the culture. However, verse 16 suggests that observation of the city was a stimulus to his preaching. Broad familiarity was not enough; he clearly wanted to understand the culture in detail.

Equally important was Paul's understanding of his own faith. His background as a student of Gamaliel ensured that he was very familiar with the Jewish Scriptures. But earlier chapters in Acts make it clear that he had also devoted several years to studying and reflecting on the Christian faith.

Finally, he related his understanding of the Christian faith to his understanding of Athenian culture. Thus he was able to proclaim the gospel in terms that his hearers could understand. He respected their culture: he used it, rather than the Old Testament, as the basis for his speech in the Areopagus.

He took pains to minimize the differences between them. For example, he did not launch into a theological treatise on the distinction between the Hebrew and the Hellenistic concepts of God. On the contrary, he assumed that key aspects of Hellenistic religion could be identified with the Christian faith.

However, while he minimized the differences, he did not compromise on the essentials. The climax of his speech was a call to repentance, combined with a proclamation of the death and resurrection of Jesus Christ.

The Anglican theologian Henry Chadwick contrasts Paul's approach with that of more defensive Christians:

> The apologist must minimize the gap between himself and his potential converts. Very different is the psychological attitude of the defender of orthodoxy; he must make as wide as possible the distance between authentic Christianity and deviationist sects against whose teaching the door must be closed with all firmness.[1]

(b) A biblical principle for Christian mission

The example set by Paul in his Areopagus speech is the basis for the fundamental principle of mission which he enunciates later in his correspondence with the Corinthian church:

> though I am free from all men, I have made myself a slave

to all, that I might win the more. To the Jews I became as a Jew, in order to win Jews; to those under the law I became as one under the law – though not being myself under the law – that I might win those under the law. To those outside the law I became as one outside the law – not being without law toward God but under the law of Christ – that I might win those outside the law. To the weak I became weak, that I might win the weak. I have become all things to all men, that I might by all means save some. (1 Cor. 9: 19–22)

Paul calls Christians to enter into the world and experience of the people to whom they would proclaim the gospel. Human nature is such that we respond more readily to people who are like us in behaviour and lifestyle; who speak the same language and use the same concepts. Like witnesses most effectively to like.

However, similarity must not be allowed to slip into identity. Paul describes his approach as being governed by the law of Christ. In other words, it is a tightrope act: minimizing the differences in order to communicate more effectively while, at the same time, refusing to compromise on matters of Christian principle.

Thus, there were three options open to the early Church in its mission to Hellenistic culture: compromise, reaction, or dialogue. Some compromised in their attempts to convey Christian truth in the language and concepts of Hellenistic philosophy: several of the major heresies faced by the Church were failures of this kind. Others reacted against Hellenistic culture, retreating into an arid sectarianism. This can already be seen in the pages of the New Testament in the form of Paul's Jewish Christian opponents. However, mainline Christianity engaged in a continuing dialogue with the culture: a dialogue which resulted in the transformation of Hellenistic culture.

The same options are open whenever Christian missionaries encounter a new culture. They can react against it, demanding that converts deny their background in favour of a 'Christian culture' (usually an amalgam of Christianity and the missionaries' parent culture). They can compromise (probably unwittingly) as they attempt to engage with the new culture. Or they can enter into the kind of dialogue alluded to above.

(c) What is dialogue?

'Dialogue' is often used as a euphemism for 'compromise': its goal is assumed to be agreement.

It is true that some dialogues do end in agreement. But there is nothing in the dictionary definition of the word to suggest that this is inevitable. Indeed the literary dialogues which form an important part of our philosophical heritage indicate a very different goal: that of mutual understanding.

Dialogue is conversation between two (or more) people. In essence, it is the verbal expression of a personal relationship. Genuine dialogue requires that at least two voices be heard. If I am to engage in dialogue I must be prepared honestly to express my own views – I must not deceive the other person by saying what I think they want to hear. However, I must also be willing to hear the other person's point of view; and I must persist until I understand. Above all, I must not, by my words or my attitude, indicate that only certain points of view are acceptable. Thus genuine dialogue entails mutual trust and respect.

Clearly such mutual trust is something which needs to be built up. Few of us are able to create such an atmosphere on our first meeting with a complete stranger. Thus dialogue may be regarded as a process or a journey. A friend of mine suggests that there are five landmarks on this journey: listening, understanding, distinguishing, evaluating and responding.[2]

Dialogue is a commitment to a shared exploration of the truth. Such an exploration must be open-ended. If either party lays down at the outset that only a particular outcome is acceptable (or if some compromise position is demanded) the exploration is not genuine dialogue.

2. CLEARING THE WAY

All cross-cultural evangelism requires certain essential preliminary work. The effort put into the training of overseas missionaries indicates that this is partly recognized by the Christian
churches. However, the virtual absence of similar training for
mission to the cultures within our own society reveals a serious
blindspot.

The situation in the UK (as throughout the First World)
today is that every Christian could be a cross-cultural evangel-
ist. There has been a tremendous proliferation of minority
and alternative cultures. The New Age is merely one of many
alternatives, albeit an important one. Such a situation demands
that we take Christian education within the churches more
seriously.

There are three ways in which churches should be preparing
Christians for cross-cultural evangelism: knowledge of the faith,
knowledge of the other culture, and experience of the faith.

(a) A mature Christian faith

All of us are called to seek to understand our faith to the limits
of our intellectual capacity: to love the Lord with all our mind
(Mark 12:30).

This will involve a growing knowledge of the Bible. But it
also involves making some effort to become familiar with
Christian theology. Theology shows us how the gospel has been
expressed in different cultural contexts in the past. It helps us
to distinguish what in the other person's culture is actually at
odds with Christianity and what is merely unfamiliar. As we
reflect on our own attempts to preach the gospel or witness,
theology is also a valuable tool for self-criticism.

(b) Orientation to the alien culture

Every missionary to a foreign culture undergoes a preliminary
process of orientation. They have to learn the language. They
also have to digest a tremendous amount of background infor-

mation about the history, politics, culture, and everyday customs of the people to whom they have been sent.

Such an orientation is essential for an initial understanding of any foreign culture whether you are a missionary to Muslims in India or a missionary to New Agers in London. If this book is able to provide Christians with such an orientation with respect to the New Age it will have served its purpose.

The purpose of such orientations is not to provide missionaries with everything they need to know about the culture. On the contrary, it would be more accurate to say that orientation lays bare the missionary's ignorance: it confronts you with how little you know about the culture.

Thus it combats the false generalizations and myths with which we protect ourselves from another culture. It helps us overcome our stereotypes of members of that culture.

(c) Learning to love

A living and growing experience of the Christian faith is another essential prerequisite for cross-cultural evangelism. Our experience of the triune God must be one that affects every aspect of our life including our attitude to others.

The dialogue approach to evangelism is dependent upon the building up of personal relationships. False motives will rapidly be revealed. Attempts at dialogue with New Agers will not ring true if our real motive is to undermine the New Age, or to fill the pews of our church with ex-New Agers.

It requires that we are growing in Christian love. Such love is unconditional. This does not mean that it is blind or uncritical. It does mean that we should not place any conditions on our care for the other person. Such conditions may turn evangelism into emotional blackmail. A test of unconditional love might be to ask yourself, 'Would I still care for this person if he or she made a conscious decision not to become a Christian after hearing my explanations of the faith?'

Such love is also practical. People who have become dissatisfied with the New Age may need considerable emotional support. If they have just left one of the more authoritarian new religious movements, they may require shelter and much practical help as they readjust to the larger society.

3. LEARNING TO LISTEN

(a) Every person is unique

We are all unique: we have our own unique life history; our own unique cultural background (no two of us have read precisely the same books, listened to the same music, or appreciated the same works of art in precisely the same way); our own unique religious experience; our own unique combination of personality traits and psychological preferences. If you were to ask fifty Christians what Christianity means to them personally, you would get fifty different answers.

The New Age is even more diverse than Christianity. Every New Ager has his or her own unique set of beliefs. The generalizations of a book such as this may be helpful for initial orientation. But to communicate effectively with individual New Agers you must find out more precisely what they believe. This requires careful listening.

(b) Getting into a world-view

Before you can express the gospel in terms that an individual New Ager will readily understand, you must have some idea of the shape of their personal beliefs. What does the New Age mean to them? What concepts do they use and how do they use them? What are their hopes, fears, and anxieties?

Other key questions (to ask yourself) might include: What do they think about the activities that make up everyday life (work, wages, and economics)? How do they relate the public world to their private life? What is their attitude to play (sport, art, entertainment)? What view do they take of various human relationships (family structures, social relationships, politics, and authority structures, our relationship with nature and with spiritual realms and beings)? What is knowledge and how do they come by it? What sense, if any, do they make of suffering, sickness, death, and evil? Last but not least, what or whom do they worship (what do they regard as ultimate reality)?

(c) Understanding

This is easily taken for granted when talking to people who share the same language. However, Christians and New Agers may share words but use them in very different ways.

One way of checking that you have, in fact, understood something is to put it in your own words and repeat it back to the other person. Asking them whether they agree will soon highlight areas of mutual misunderstanding.

(d) Discernment

This is where knowledge of the Bible and Christian theology is invaluable. Faced with an unfamiliar assertion about God or life, you have to be able to assess whether it is compatible with Christian belief, neutral, or incompatible. This is not simply a mechanical matter of checking the other person's beliefs off against a clear-cut list of doctrines: beliefs tend to be inter-related in a dynamic fashion.

Discernment is needed in responding to New Age criticisms of Christianity. It is dangerous to assume that all criticisms are misunderstandings or malicious caricatures: some of their complaints about the Church are legitimate. But, it is equally dangerous to accept all criticisms of Christianity: background knowledge is needed to discern which are ill-founded.

We need to be able to discern points at which we can agree with New Agers. The example of Paul in Athens shows how important such common ground was to his preaching of the gospel. But, like Paul, we also need to be clear about what are the sticking points.

4. READINESS TO REPENT

(a) The challenge of the New Age

The New Age phenomenon is, in part, a legitimate reaction against certain aspects of post-Enlightenment thought. For example it questions the sufficiency of human reason as the final arbiter of truth and the ultimate means of obtaining knowledge. It is also critical of the mind-body dualism which has dominated much of western thought and the tendency to reductionism.

The New Age is also an indictment of twentieth-century institutional Christianity. Some commentators try to evade this issue by suggesting that New Agers have never heard the gospel. But this is not borne out by even a cursory examination of the backgrounds of leading New Agers. Sir George Trevelyan describes himself as an Anglican.[3] Shirley Maclaine was brought up as a Southern Baptist.[4] J. Z. Knight, the internationally known channel for Ramtha, came from a Christian fundamentalist home.[5] Surveys of the religious backgrounds of American Neo-Pagans suggest that about 70 per cent come from Christian homes (40 per cent Protestant).[6]

For many New Agers, the Church has been tried and found wanting. Their reasons for abandoning the religion of their youth suggest that, at root, the failure of the Church has been a failure to maintain the dialogue between gospel and culture of which I have already spoken. They may have taken offence at a church which has sold out to post-Enlightenment culture. Alternatively they may have objected to the reactionary approach of a fundamentalist church.

(b) Rationalistic Christianity

A good deal of western Christianity is seriously lopsided. Because of the Enlightenment emphasis on the supremacy of human reason, the Church has tended to value the head over other aspects of what it is to be human. Thus Christians have discounted the imagination, feelings, and the body.

A corollary of this overemphasis on the head has been a

tendency to naturalism. Many Christians, including many evangelicals, are uncomfortable about the supernatural aspects of Christian faith and belief. Miracles, words of prophecy, and personal spiritual entities (angels and demons) are reinterpreted figuratively or relegated safely to the past. Similarly eschatology was for a long time overlooked as an aspect of Christian teaching.

The New Age phenomenon questions this discomfort. Here are millions of people who, dissatisfied with what the Church was saying or not saying, have sought elsewhere for accounts of spiritual realities.

The holism of the New Age is a timely reminder that Christianity too is a holistic faith. It shares with Hebrew thought a holistic concept of human fulfillment: *shalom*, the peace which includes physical and mental well-being, social justice and righteousness before God. It calls for a total response to God with hearts, minds, spirits, and bodies. And it expects that our response will affect every aspect of life at all times.

(c) Worldly Christianity

A frequent complaint against western churches is their worldliness. For many New Agers they embody the values of a materialistic culture.

This may be seen in the way in which church institutions reflect the behaviour of secular politics. The hierarchical structure of the older churches and the more bureaucratic style of newer Protestant churches both owe more to the secular institutions of the cultures from which they have emerged than to anything in the New Testament. That in itself is not a problem – it is part of the dialogue between gospel and culture. But, when churches reflect the unacceptable face of secular institutions (the cult of the personality, dishonesty, corruption, the disempowerment of the laity, the marginalization of some groups) New Agers and others are right to criticize us.

More generally, the attitudes of Christians towards others have too often reflected and condoned the worst prejudices of the dominant culture. We see this in the persistent racism of western churches. In addition to the long and inglorious history of Christian anti-Semitism, there is the churches' prejudice against blacks: biblical support for slavery, apartheid, the lack of welcome shown by British churches to Caribbean immigrants. It is also to be seen in the sexism of many Christian institutions and in the disregard for the natural world displayed by many Christians. New Agers rightly take offence at all these distortions of the Christian gospel.

5. CONFRONTATION IN LOVE

(a) Using their language

The way of dialogue is time intensive. There are no short cuts. It is not enough to preach the gospel in familiar jargon and hope that the message will get through. Many New Agers have listened to what Christians have to say but have not heard the gospel. We should not try to evade our responsibility by arguing that Satan has closed their ears. That may be so in some cases. However, in the majority of cases, it is more probable that the Christians did not bother to check that they were being understood.

We have to express the gospel in terms that New Agers can understand. As Dean Halverson points out:

> Evangelism is more than haphazardly sowing the seed of the Gospel: It is translating the message of Jesus into the language of the hearer. If you can empathize with another's view of reality, then you will be able to address the needs they feel are important. When you can speak to them from their own frame of reference, it is more likely they will listen and heed your words.[7]

For example, New Agers stress the importance of self-fulfillment and the need for personal transformation to achieve that goal. Contrary to popular opinion, Christianity also stresses self-fulfillment: Martin Luther once said that 'God became man so that man might become fully human'.[8] A desire to achieve our full human potential is something which Christians and New Agers ought to have in common. Furthermore, we can agree that this can only come about through personal transformation: there is a need for spiritual awakening.

However, we must ask whether the New Age view of personal transformation is radical enough. Does dismissing evil as illusion really address the problem? Can personal transformation be achieved by the mechanical application of certain techniques? The Bible uses the metaphor of new birth to describe it: the transformation required is so far-reaching that it is like being born again.

This raises the further question of whether we are able to transform ourselves. Can we give birth to ourselves? And if not, what agency is there to act as midwife? Many New Agers respond positively to the concept of the cosmic Christ. This is a biblical concept (e.g., Col. 1: 15–17) and we need to reclaim it as part of our Christian vocabulary. But we have to insist that the cosmic Christ is more than a myth to live by. Paul's understanding of the cosmic Christ was rooted in the historical actuality of the incarnation, death, and resurrection of Jesus of Nazareth.

How can we make the Bible more accessible to New Agers? The key is choosing the right entry point. We must be able to identify those books and passages which most directly address the hopes and fears of the person to whom we are talking. My own experience, having become a Christian after a rather isolated pilgrimage through the outer fringes of the new consciousness movement, suggests that John's Gospel and the First Letter of John may be helpful starting points. However, as always, you must beware of generalizations.

(b) An ongoing process

Dialogue is a process. It is possible that someone will become a Christian as soon as they hear what you have to say. However, if this happens, it may well be that there is already a long history of preparation behind the event.

More probably they will want to disagree with things you have said, or they will want you to clarify things. Commitment to dialogue implies that you must be prepared to listen to their response. Have they understood what you were trying to say?

Have they misunderstood because of some presupposition of which you were unaware? Or have you misled them by an inappropriate choice of words?

In all probability, you will have made some mistakes. Do not be afraid of mistakes: fear of getting it wrong is one of the major hindrances to evangelism. It is more important to make an effort to communicate than it is to achieve doctrinal correctness.

But equally important is a willingness to be critical of your efforts to communicate the gospel. This is virtually a commitment to do theology. In fact, my favourite definition of theology is 'the persistent and disciplined asking and answering of the question: Given that the Christian community has in the past said and done such-and-such, what should it say and do now?'[9] When you ask yourself, 'how could I have put it more clearly?', you are doing theology.

In the light of such self-criticism you will be able to go back to the other person, admit your mistakes, and try again. And so the process of dialogue goes on.

When you confront a person with the gospel in this way, you confront them in love. There is no element of coercion in dialogue. You are not attempting to convert them to Christianity – that, after all, is not your task but the Holy Spirit's.

Personal evangelism is more like the issuing of an invitation than indoctrination. You are inviting the other person to explore your understanding of Jesus Christ and ask what relevance this understanding has for their life. It is not dissimilar to the tactic Jesus often used – on several occasions in the Gospels he invites enquirers simply to spend time with him.

Implicit in such an approach is the necessity for an underlying lifestyle evangelism. For people to want to take this time getting to know Jesus we must have presented them with an attractive picture of Christianity. Here our lives speak far louder than our words. It is the way our faith affects our conduct of daily life, our relationships and our worship that counts.

(c) The goal

Ultimately the goal of evangelism is not to fill our churches nor even to convert people to Christianity, it is to introduce them to Jesus.

As New Agers hear the gospel freed from its bondage to old institutions, as they discover that there is something about Jesus that gives meaning to life, and as they find themselves unable to evade him, something more than personal transformation will take place.

When carried on faithfully, the dialogue between the gospel and particular cultures has always resulted in two things: the transformation of the culture and the transformation of the Church. The same will be true of our dialogue with the New Age.

Notes

For the sake of brevity, I have used the Author-Date System of references. Articles and books are referred to by surname of author (or editor) and date of publication. They may be identified by consulting the bibliography.

INTRODUCTION

1. Riddell 1991, P. 84.
2. From 'Adventure in Avalon . . .' a brochure published by *Gaia: Glastonbury Advice and Information Agency*.
3. This impression may have been created by the fact that the Festival has spawned other major events such as the Healing Arts Festival and now also has to compete with a range of local psychic fairs.

CHAPTER 1 TRANSFORMING THE BODY: HOLISTIC HEALTH IN THE NEW AGE

1. Wylie 1991, p. 116.
2. E.g., the *Il Hwa* group of companies (a major American importer of ginseng) is closely associated with Revd Sung Myung Moon.
3. Its advocates have included Dr Martyn Lloyd-Jones and Jim Elliott (the American missionary who was martyred in Ecuador in 1956).
4. Wylie 1991, p. 120.
5. Cited by Autore 1990, p. 23.
6. This is similar to the starting point of Neoplatonic cosmology (which greatly influenced the thought of St Augustine and subsequent western theologians). The key difference is that the

Neoplatonic scheme does not develop a self-perpetuating dynamic duality but envisages the whole of reality as a process of defection from and return to the Absolute.

7. E.g., physicians in China today often use acupuncture as a supplement to conventional anaesthetics rather than an alternative.

8. Interestingly he did so by exposing groups of students to strong visual imagery: antibody levels increased in groups who watched a film about Mother Theresa and decreased in those who watched a documentary about the Nazis.

9. These include faith healing, psychic healing, holistic healing, esoteric healing, natural healing, and healing.

10. Thomas 1978, p. 339.

CHAPTER 2 TRANSFORMING THE MIND: PSYCHOANALYSIS AND THE NEW AGE

1. Jung 1983, p. 173.
2. Wittgenstein 1966, p. 51.
3. Jung 1983, pp. 200f.
4. Franz 1964, p. 161.
5. Jung 1976, pp. 36f.
6. Ibid., p. 45.
7. Ibid., p. 61.
8. Garrison 1982, p. 131.
9. Jung 1976, p. 45.
10. Franz 1964, p. 163.
11. Garrison 1982, p. 143.
12. Jung 1983, pp. 413f.
13. Garrison 1982, p. 140.
14. A survey of leading American New Agers revealed that Jung was the second most important influence on their ideas after Teilhard de Chardin (Ferguson 1981, pp. 418–20).
15. Jung 1983, p. 405.
16. Heyt 1976, p. 69.
17. Storr 1976, pp. 15–47.
18. Cited by Drury 1989, p. 33.
19. Maslow 1979, p. 264.
20. Toffler 1981, p. 366.
21. Rhinehart 1976, p. 217.
22. Silva & Miele 1977, pp. 85–8.
23. Cited by Drury 1989, p. 39.

CHAPTER 3 TRANSFORMING THE SPIRIT

1. Lossky 1957, pp. 8f.
2. Guptara & Osmaston 1987, p. 5.
3. Jung 1982, p. 81.
4. Adler 1986, p. 447.
5. Thomas 1978, pp. 332f.
6. Keith Thomas cites a number of divinatory practices in sixteenth- and seventeenth-century England but Tarot reading is not one of them.
7. 'Magick' is the spelling preferred by modern occultists to distinguish what they practise from 'magic' or conjuring of the stage variety.
8. E.g., Matthews, C. & J. 1985, 1986.
9. Melton 1990, p. 133.
10. Warren-Clarke 1987, p. 19.

CHAPTER 4 TRANSFORMING THE WORLD: THE NEW AGE AND SOCIETY

1. Ferguson 1981, p. 191.
2. Cited by Melton 1990, p. 160.
3. Ibid., p. 324.
4. Ibid., p. 323.
5. E.g., Starhawk 1990.
6. Adler 1986, pp. 206–22.
7. E.g., Merchant 1979, Primavesi 1991.
8. Cole et al. 1990, p. 95.
9. Pepper 1991, Chapter 1.
10. Cited in Porritt & Winner 1988, pp. 236, 238.
11. Passmore 1980, p. ix.
12. E.g., Albanese 1990.
13. E.g., Marks 1989, p. 181.
14. Drane 1991, p. 171.
15. Adler 1986, p. 285.
16. Ibid., p. 445.
17. Strachan, J. 1990, p. 14.
18. Ferguson 1981, p. 287.
19. Clause 1, Section 2a.
20. Harris 1987, p. 8.
21. Hall 1987, pp. 44–6; Herzog 1982, pp. 5–29.
22. Raban 1987, p. 18; Hall 1987, p. 41.

23. Raban 1987, p. 20.
24. Hall 1987, p. 48.
25. Jung 1936.
26. Ebeling 1970, p. 138.

CHAPTER 5 TRANSFORMING SCIENCE?

1. Adler 1986, p. 392.
2. Ibid., p. 396.
3. Ferguson 1981, pp. 418–20.
4. Teilhard 1969, p. 68.
5. Ibid., pp. 119f.
6. Teilhard 1974, p. 146.
7. Lovelock 1979, p. 11.
8. Lovelock 1988, p. xvi.
9. Ibid., p. 8.
10. Sheldrake 1990, p. 129.
11. Trevelyan 1986, p. 68.
12. Russell 1982, p. 95.
13. Ibid., p. 78.
14. Roszak 1981, p. 65.
15. Out of nearly 1200 volumes on my database of New Age publications only 7 make any substantial reference to the Gaia hypothesis. As of December 1990 the journal *Kindred Spirit* had never run an article on the subject. Another British New Age journal, *Resurgence*, published an article by Lovelock in October 1990 – but this was merely a reprint of an earlier article in *Nature*.
16. E.g., Pedler 1979, Sahtouris 1989.
17. Sheldrake 1990, p. 88.
18. Ferguson 1981, p. 373.
19. Capra 1976, p. 134.
20. Ibid., p. 65.
21. Ibid., p. 167.
22. Ibid., p. 197.
23. E.g., ibid., pp. 65, 212.
24. Zukav 1980, p. 88.
25. Capra 1976, p. 292.
26. E.g., Barrow & Tipler 1986, pp. 458–89.
27. Melton 1990, p. xxx.

CHAPTER 6 BEYOND REASON: KNOWLEDGE AND WISDOM IN THE NEW AGE

1. Lewis 1965, p. 41.
2. Copleston 1947, p. 93.
3. By contrast, eastern Orthodoxy, at its best, derives personhood from the concept of a relationality which emerges from the doctrine of the Trinity.
4. Rajneesh 1977, p. 18.
5. Ferguson 1981, pp. 79f.
6. Capra 1976, pp. 26–45.
7. Ferguson 1981, p. 373.
8. Capra 1976, p. 29.
9. Cited by Capra 1976, p. 35.
10. Adler 1986, p. 160.
11. Wilgus 1976, p. 32.

CHAPTER 7 THE ONE AND THE MANY: REALITY IN THE NEW AGE

1. Cited by Miller 1990, p. 65.
2. Ferguson 1981, p. 25.
3. Trevelyan 1981, p. 19.
4. Ibid., p. 118.
5. Capra 1982, p. 317.
6. Ferguson 1981, p. 382.
7. Sheldrake 1990, p. 189.
8. Sahtouris 1989, p. 27.
9. Trevelyan 1986, p. 69.
10. Ferguson 1973, p. 60.
11. Sire 1977, p. 177.
12. Gilbert Ryle cited by Barbour 1966, p. 353.
13. Shire 1977, p. 178.
14. Barbour 1966, p. 163.
15. Trevelyan 1981, p. 14.
16. E.g., Spangler 1971, p. 16.
17. Notably *Chipko Andolan* (the Hug-the-trees Movement), an environmentalist group based on Gandhian principles.
18. E.g., Tuan 1970.
19. Starhawk 1979, p. 25.
20. Lilly 1972, p. 39.
21. Jung 1983, p. 206.

22. This emerged during discussions with Mr C. Szurko (Director of Dialogcentre UK) following the 1991 Festival of Mind, Body and Spirit. However, further investigation is required to confirm the existence of such a trend.

CHAPTER 8 SAGES AND SUPERMEN: NEW AGE VISIONS OF HUMANITY

1. Ash & Hewitt 1990, p. 182.
2. Starhawk 1990, p. 13.
3. Ibid., p. 13.
4. Spangler 1971, p. 22.
5. Starhawk 1979, p. 81.
6. This quotation comes from a document entitled *Are Such Things Done on Albion's Shore?* privately circulated in 1987 by a Jewish New Ager to warn people about fascist elements within the British New Age Movement.
7. This statement was made during the course of a lecture entitled 'The Rising Tide of Love' given at the Festival for Mind, Body and Spirit in London, 24th May 1991.
8. Ash & Hewitt 1990, p. 181.
9. Ibid., pp. 181, 182.
10. Molnar 1987, p. 26.
11. Matthews, C. & J. 1986, p. 26.
12. Ibid., p. 101.
13. Freedman 1981, pp. 11, 12.
14. Nietzsche 1977, pp. 202f.
15. Ibid., p. 216.
16. Ibid., p. 203.

CHAPTER 9 CHRIST IN THE NEW AGE

1. Spink 1989, p. 1.
2. Cobb 1975, p. 76.
3. Melton 1990, p. 47.
4. Kuthumi 1976, p. 103.
5. Prophet 1975, p. 125.
6. Trevelyan 1981, pp. 27, 29.
7. Ibid., p. 93.
8. Ibid., p. 32.

9. Ibid., p. 34.
10. Romarheim 1988, p. 207.

CHAPTER 10 TRANSFORMING CHRISTIANITY: NEW AGE IN THE CHURCHES

1. E.g., Strachan, G. 1985, pp. 110–22.
2. From a letter to *Green Christians*, Feb.-Apr. 1989, p. 11.
3. Cole et al. 1990, p. 52.
4. Two of its three directors, William Bloom and Sabrina Dearborn, are regular speakers at Findhorn and Ms Dearborn is a former Findhorn focaliser.
5. Cited by Cole et al. 1990, p. 48.
6. Ibid., p. 49.
7. Spink 1991, p. 113.
8. Spink 1983, p. 16.
9. Spink 1980, p. 52.
10. Spink 1991, p. 99.
11. Spink 1980, p. 18.
12. E.g., Bloom 1990, pp. 123, 125.
13. I distinguish Fox's creation-centred spirituality from *creation spirituality* (which I understand as a blanket term for any spirituality in which we seek to meet God in creation). The latter may be perfectly orthodox as I have sought to demonstrate in my Grove Book *Meeting God in Creation*.
14. His ideas are set out in great detail in Fox 1983.
15. Ibid., pp. 38f.
16. Fox 1981, p. 79.
17. Fox 1983, pp. 28f.
18. Ibid., p . 315.

CHAPTER 11 BUILDING UP THE DIVIDING WALLS OF HOSTILITY: THE WAY OF REACTION

1. Baer 1989, pp. 78f.
2. From correspondence with Peter Elliott, editor of ORCRO Magazine.
3. Cumbey 1983, p. 61.
4. Ibid., p. 39.
5. E.g., ibid., pp. 55f.

6. Ibid., p. 84. *Planetary Citizens* was founded in the early 1970s to prepare for the coming of a global culture. It is one of the most prestigious New Age organizations, including amongst its founders U. Thant (a former secretary general of the United Nations).
7. Ibid., p. 90.
8. Ibid., p. 258.
9. Ibid., p. 156.
10. Roman Catholic involvement is a major theme of Livesey 1986.
11. Cumbey 1983, p. 168. Compare Wilkinson 1980, p. 222.
12. Cumbey 1983, p. 73.
13. Riddell 1991, p. 64.
14. Cole et al. 1990, p. 107. My emphasis.
15. Livesey 1986, p. 110.
16. E.g., Wilcock 1975, pp. 122–8.
17. Eco 1989, p. 619.
18. Ibid., p. 619.
19. E.g., DeParrie & Pride, 1989, associate the New Age with human sacrifice (p. 42) and sexual deviation (p. 70) amongst other things.
20. Sire 1980, p. 18.
21. DeParrie & Pride 1989, pp. 115–17.
22. Ibid., pp. 197–200.
23. Rita Bennett and Richard Foster both stress the value of prayerful visualization. However, since its condemnation by conspiracy theorist Dave Hunt, key members of the charismatic movement such as John Wimber have tended to play down its value.

CHAPTER 12 CONFRONTATION IN LOVE: THE WAY OF DIALOGUE

1. Chadwick 1955, p. 275.
2. Szurko 1988, p. 1.
3. Spink 1991, p. 2.
4. Melton 1990, p. 270.
5. Chandler 1989, p. 55.
6. Adler 1986, p. 444.
7. Hoyt 1987, p. 207.
8. Primavesi 1991, p. 97.
9. Jenson 1973, p. vii.

Bibliography

Adler, M., *Drawing Down the Moon: Witches, Druids, Goddess-Worshippers and other Pagans in America Today*, revised edition (Boston, MA: Beacon Press, 1986).

Albanese, C. L., *Nature Religion in America: From the Algonquin Indians to the New Age* (Chicago: University of Chicago Press, 1990).

Ash, D. & Hewitt, P., *Science of the Gods: Reconciling Mystery and Matter* (Bath: Gateway Books, 1990).

Autore, M., 'The Contemplative Way of Tai Chi Chuan', *Areopagus 3*, no. 3 (1990), pp. 21–5.

Barbour, I. G., *Issues in Science and Religion* (London: SCM, 1966).

Barrow, J. & Tipler, F., *The Anthropic Cosmological Principle* (Oxford: OUP, 1986).

Baer, R. N., *Inside the New Age Nightmare* (Lafayette, Louisiana: Huntington House, 1989).

Bloom, W., *Sacred Times: A New Approach to Festivals* (Forres: Findhorn Press, 1990).

Capra, F., *The Tao of Physics* (London: Fontana, 1976).
The Turning Point: Science, Society and the Rising Culture (London: Wildwood House, 1982).

Chadwick, H., 'All Things to All Men' in M. Black (ed.) *New Testament Studies, Vol. 1* (Cambridge: CUP, 1955).

Chandler, R., *Understanding the New Age* (Milton Keynes: Word Books, 1989).

Cobb, J. B., *Christ in a Pluralistic Age* (Philadelphia: Westminster Press, 1975).

Cole, M. et al., *What Is The New Age?* (London: Hodders, 1990).

Copleston, F., *A History of Philosophy, Vol. 1: Greece and Rome* (Burns Oates, 1947).

Cumbey, C., *Hidden Dangers of the Rainbow: The New Age Move-*

ment and our Coming Age of Barbarism (Shreveport, Louisiana: Huntington House, 1983).

DeParrie, P. & Pride, M., *Ancient Empires of the New Age* (Westchester, ILL: Crossway Books, 1989).

Drane, J., *What is the New Age Saying to the Church?* (London: Marshall Pickering, 1991).

Drury, N., *The Elements of Human Potential* (Shaftesbury: Element, 1989).

Ebeling, G., *Luther: An introduction to his thought* (London: Collins, 1970).

Eco, U., *Foucault's Pendulum* (London: Secker & Warburg, 1989).

Ferguson, M., *The Brain Revolution: Frontiers of Mind Research* (New York: Taplinger Publ. Co., 1973).
The Aquarian Conspiracy: Personal and Social Transformation in the 1980s (London: RKP, 1981).

Fox, M., *Whee! We, Wee All the Way Home: A Guide to Sensual, Prophetic Spirituality* (Santa Fe: Bear & Co., 1981).
Original Blessing. A Primer in Creation Spirituality (Santa Fe: Bear & Co, 1983).

Franz, M-L. von, 'The Process of Individuation' in Jung & von Franz (eds.), *Man and his Symbols* (London: Aldus, 1964), pp. 158–229.

Freedman, R., *Hermann Hesse: Pilgrim of Crisis* (London: Sphere Books, 1981).

Garrison, J., *The Darkness of God: Theology after Hiroshima* (London: SCM, 1982).

Guptara, P. & Osmaston, A., *Yoga – A Christian Option?* (Nottingham: Grove Books, 1987).

Hall, E., 'Fantasy in Religious Education: A Psychological Perspective', *British Journal of Religious Education* 10, 1987), pp. 41–8.

Harris, M., 'Fantasy: Entrance Into Inwardness', *British Journal of Religious Education* 10 (1987), pp. 8–14.

Herzog, S., *Joy in the Classroom* (Boulder Creek, CA: University of the Trees Press, 1982).

Heyt, V. von der, *Prospects for the Soul: Soundings in Jungian Psychology and Religion* (London: DLT, 1976).

Hoyt, K., (ed.), *The New Age Rage* (Old Tappan, NJ: Revell, 1987).

Jenson, R., *Story and Promise: A Brief Theology of the Gospel about Jesus* (Philadelphia: Fortress Press, 1973).

Jung, C. G., 'Wotan' (1936) in *Collected Works Vol. 10* (Princeton University Press, 1970).
The Portable Jung, ed. J. Campbell (Harmondsworth: Penguin, 1976).

Psychology and the East (London: RKP, 1982).

Memories, Dreams, Reflections (London: Fontana, 1983).

Kuthumi, *Studies of the Human Aura* (Los Angeles: Summit University Press, 1976).

Lewis, H. D., *Philosophy of Religion* (London: English Universities Press, 1965).

Lilly, J., *The Centre of the Cyclone: An autobiography of inner space* (New York: Julian Press, 1972).

Livesey, R., *Understanding the New Age* (Chichester: New Wine Press, 1986).

Lovelock, J., *Gaia: A New Look at Life on Earth* (Oxford: OUP, 1979).

The Ages of Gaia: A Biography of our Living Planet (Oxford: OUP, 1988).

Lossky, V., *The Mystical Theology of the Eastern Church* (Cambridge: James Clarke & Co, 1957).

Marks, L., *Living With Vision: Reclaiming the Power of the Heart* (Indianapolis: Knowledge Systems, 1989).

Maslow, A., *The Farther Reaches of Human Nature* (New York: Penguin, 1979).

Matthews, C. & J., *The Western Way: A Practical Guide to the Western Mystery Tradition, Vol. 1: The Native Tradition* (London: Arkana, 1985).

The Western Way: A Practical Guide to the Western Mystery Tradition: Vol. 2: The Hermetic Tradition (London: Arkana 1986).

Melton, G., *New Age Encyclopedia* (Detroit: Gale Research, 1990).

Merchant, C., *The Death of Nature: Women, ecology and the scientific revolution* (San Francisco: Harper & Row, 1979).

Miller, E., *A Crash Course on the New Age Movement* (Eastbourne: Monarch, 1990).

Molnar, T., *The Pagan Temptation* (Grand Rapids, Michigan: Eerdmans, 1987).

Nietzsche, F., *A Nietzsche Reader*, selected by R. J. Hollingdale (Harmondsworth: Penguin, 1977).

Passmore, J., *Man's Responsibility for Nature*, revised edition (London: Duckworth, 1980).

Pedler, K., *The Quest for Gaia: A book of changes* (London: Souvenir Press, 1979).

Pepper, D., *Communes and the Green Vision: Counterculture, Lifestyle and the New Age* (London: Green Print, 1991).

Porritt, J. & Winner, D., *The Coming of the Greens* (London: Collins, 1988).

Primavesi, A., *From Apocalypse to Genesis: Ecology, Feminism and Christianity* (Tunbridge Wells: Burns & Oates, 1991).

Prophet, M. & E., *Climb the Highest Mountain* (Los Angeles: Summit University Press, 1975).

Raban, K., 'Guided Imagery: Young Children and Religious Education', *British Journal of Religious Education* 10 (1987), pp. 15–22.

Rajneesh, *I Am the Gate* (New York: Harper & Row, 1977).

Rhinehart, L., *The Book of EST* (New York: Holt, Rinehart & Wilson, 1976).

Riddell, C., *The Findhorn Community: Creating a Human Identity for the 21st Century* (Forres: Findhorn Press, 1991).

Romarheim, A., 'The Aquarian Christ', *Bulletin of John Rylands Library* 70 (1988), pp. 197–207.

Roszak, T., *Person/Planet: The Creative Disintegration of Industrial Society* (London: Granada, 1981).

Russell, P., *The Awakening Earth: Our Next Evolutionary Leap* (London: RKP, 1982).

Sahtouris, E., *Gaia: The Human Journey from Chaos to Cosmos* (New York: Simon & Schuster, 1989).

Sheldrake, R., *The Rebirth of Nature: The Greening of Science and of God* (London: Century, 1990).

Silva, J. & Miele, P., *The Silva Mind Control Method* (New York: Simon & Schuster, 1977).

Sire, J., *The Universe Next Door: A Guide to World Views* (Leicester: IVP, 1977).

Scripture Twisting (Downers Grove, Ill.: IVP, 1980).

Spangler, D., *Revelation: The Birth of a New Age* (Forres: Findhorn Press, 1971).

Spink, P., *Spiritual Man in a New Age* (London: DLT, 1980).

The End of an Age (Tunbridge Wells: Omega Trust, 1983).

'What of the Future', *Omega News* 38 (Summer 1989), pp. 1–2.

A Christian in the New Age (London: DLT, 1991).

Starhawk, *The Spiral Dance: A Rebirth of the Ancient Religion of the Great Goddess* (San Francisco: Harper & Row, 1979).

Dreaming the Dark: Magic, Sex and Politics, revised edition (London: Unwin Hyman, 1990).

Storr, A., *The Dynamics of Creation* (Harmondsworth: Penguin, 1976).

Strachan, G., *Christ and the Cosmos* (Dunbar: Labarum, 1985).

Strachan, J., 'Who is Frank Peretti?' An interview in *Christian Bookseller Review* (March 1990), pp. 12–15.

Szurko, C., ' "Dialogue" Why?' (London: Dialogcentre UK, 1988).

Teilhard de Chardin, P., *The Future of Man* (London: Fontana, 1969). *Let Me Explain* (London: Fontana, 1974).

Thomas, K., *Religion and the Decline of Magic: Studies in popular beliefs in sixteenth- and seventeenth-century England* (Harmondsworth: Penguin, 1978).

Toffler, A., *The Third Wave* (New York: Bantam, 1981).

Trevelyan, G., *Operation Redemption: A Vision of Hope in an Age of Turmoil* (Wellingborough: Turnstone, 1981). *Summons to a High Crusade* (Forres: Findhorn Press, 1986).

Tuan, Y-F., 1970 'Our Treatment of the Environment in Ideal and Actuality', *American Scientist* 58, no. 3 (1970), pp. 244–9.

Warren-Clarke, L., *The Way of the Goddess: A Manual for Wiccan Initiation* (Bridport: Prism Press, 1987).

Wilcock, M., *I Saw Heaven Opened: The Message of Revelation* (London: IVP, 1975).

Wilgus, N., 'An Interview with Robert Anton Wilson', *Science Fiction Review* 5, no. 2 (1976), p. 32.

Wilkinson, L., *Earthkeeping: Christian Stewardship of Natural Resources* (Grand Rapids, Michigan: Eerdmans, 1980).

Wittgenstein, L., *Lectures and Conversations on Aesthetics, Psychology & Religious Belief* (Oxford: Blackwell, 1966).

Wylie, P., *The Holistic Network Directory 1991/92* (London: Holistic Network, 1991).

Zukav, G., *The Dancing Wu Li Masters: An Overview of the New Physics* (London: Fontana, 1980).

Appendix:
Some Useful Addresses

INFORM (Information Network Focus on Religious Movements), Lionel Robbins Building, 10 Portugal Street, London, WC2A 2HD (071–831 4990): a useful source of objective, up-to-date information about new religious movements.

DIALOGCENTRE UK, BM DialogCentre, London WC1N 3XX: offers information on new religious movements from an explicitly Christian perspective; it also offers counselling to members of new religious movements (on a voluntary basis: it is opposed to forcible 'de-programming').

Critical mass P61

  definition of P62

Networking - Computer term
    ↳ New Age terminology } 63

A theoretical explanation for the origin of humanity P83